Sun Tzu's

THE
ART
OF
WAR

Plus

Its
Amazing
Secrets

The Keys to Strategy

IndependentPublisher.com
Highlighted Title
★ READ THIS BOOK! ★

Gary Gagliardi

Ancient Secrets Revealed!

2,500 hundred years ago, Sun Tzu wrote the history's most powerful work on strategy. Even in English translation, some of its genius shines through, but it takes years of studying the original Chinese to master its many secrets. The purpose of this work is to make it possible for English readers to easily appreciate and see some of the hidden power of Sun Tzu's *The Art of War*. To accomplish this task, this book offers a number of innovations.

• The complete English translation of Sun Tzu's *The Art of War* appears on left-hand pages with sections and lines numbered for quick reference.

• The facing, right-hand pages explain the hidden secrets of each stanza in parallel with the text.

• Chinese words are explained to highlight the differences between Sun Tzu's concepts and the simpler English terms used in translation.

• The beginning of each chapter shows illustrations of key conceptual relationships using the traditional Chinese system of diagramming called *yao*.

• The larger design and pattern of the work is explained because that context is what gives much of the text its meaning.

• The cultural metaphors used by Sun Tzu to express his concepts are explained so that the most poetic sections can be readily understood.

• The glossary of key concepts in the back of the book uses Sun Tzu's definitions to describe the relationships among ideas.

The innovations taken together make this book into a invaluable tool for understanding and mastering the power of *The Art of War*.

Dedicated to an amazing woman,
my mother, Anita, (1919-2013)

孫子兵法

Sun Tzu's

THE
ART
OF
WAR

Plus

Its Amazing Secrets
The Keys to Strategy

Multicultural Nonfiction
Independent Publishers
Book Award
2005 - Finalist

The Second Book in the Award-Winning Series

Mastering Sun Tzu's Text

Amazing Secrets is the second volume in a three-book series revealing and explaining Sun Tzu's text of *The Art of War*. The other two books in the series are described below. All three of these books have won book award recognition, as have many of Gary's other works on strategy (see facing page).

The first book in the series, *Sun Tzu's The Art of War Plus The Ancient Chinese Revealed,* shows formulaic nature of the original Chinese ideograms. It shows the original Chinese with a transliteration of each Chinese character. This transliteration is shown side-by-side with the English sentence translation on the left-hand page of this book. This work won the Independent Publishers Book Award as the Best Multicultural Nonfiction work in 2003.

The third book in the series, *The Art of War Plus The Warrior Class*, is a 320-page study guide for the text. The book offers a one-page lesson based on each stanza of *The Art of War*. These lesson put *The Art of War* text to work in the modern world and was the beginning of our training program in Sun Tzu's strategy. This book won award recognition as one of the best self-help books of the year from *Forward Magazine*, the leading magazine of the publishing industry.

Award Recognition for *Art of War* Strategy Books
by Gary Gagliardi

The Golden Key to Strategy

Psychology/Self-Help
Ben Franklin
Book Award
2006 - Winner

*The Art of War Plus
The Ancient Chinese Revealed*

Multicultural Nonfiction
Independent Publishers
Book Award
2003 - Winner

*Making Money by Speaking:
The Spokesperson Strategy*

Career
Foreword Magazine
Book of the Year
2007 - Finalist

Strategy for Sales Managers

Business
Independent Publishers
Book Award
2006 - Semi-Finalist

*The Warrior Class:
306 Lessons in Strategy*

Self-Help
Foreword Magazine
Book of the Year
2005 - Finalist

Strategy Against Terror

Philosophy
Foreword Magazine
Book of the Year
2005 - Finalist

*The Ancient Bing-fa:
Martial Arts Strategy*

Sports
Foreword Magazine
Book of the Year
2007 - Finalist

*The Art of War Plus
The Art of Marketing*

Business
Ben Franklin
Book Award
2004 - Finalist

The Warrior's Apprentice

Youth Nonfiction
Independent Publishers
Book Award
2006 - Semi-Finalist

孫子兵法

Sun Tzu's
THE
ART
OF
WAR

Plus

Its Amazing Secrets
The Keys to Strategy

by Gary Gagliardi

Science of Strategy Institute
Clearbridge Publishing

Published by
Science of Strategy Institute, Clearbridge Publishing
suntzus.com   scienceofstrategy.org

Fourth Edition
Copyright 1999, 2000, 2001, 2003, 2004, 2011, 2014 Gary Gagliardi
ISBN 978-1-929194-91-9 (13-digit) 1-929194-91-9 (10-digit)

Manufactured in the United States of America.
Original interior and cover graphic design by Dana and Jeff Wincapaw.
Original Chinese calligraphy by Tsai Yung, Green Dragon Arts, www.greendragonarts.com.

Publisher's Cataloging-in-Publication Data
Sun-tzu, 6th cent. B.C.
    [Sun-tzu ping fa, English]
    The art of war plus its amazing secrets / Sun Tzu; Gary Gagliardi.
    p. 192 cm. 23
    Includes glossary of key Chinese concepts
    1. Military art and science - Early works to 1800. 2. Competition. I. Gagliardi, Gary 1951— . II.
Title.
U101'.S9513 2003
355'.02 — dc19
                              Library of Congress Catalog Card Number: 2001090321

Clearbridge Publishing's books may be purchased for business, for any promotional use,
or for special sales. Please contact:

Science of Strategy Institute
2829 Linkview Dr.
Las Vegas, NV 89134
garyg@suntzus.com

Contents

The Art of War Plus

Its Amazing Secrets

Preface

The Beginnings of the Science of Strategy

When this book was first published at the turn of the millennium, it was the foundation of what we now call Sun Tzu's Science of Strategy. Since then, we have developed its concepts in much more detail, especially in the nine volumes of our *Sun Tzu's Art of War Playbook*. However, this book provides the conceptual foundation for all the work that follows and an important connection point to traditional Chinese philosophy.

Our language for discussing Sun Tzu's concepts has evolved over this time, but the graphical portrayals in this work are more important than the terminology we use. After all, much of our work has been adapting Sun Tzu's concepts into the different terminologies of various competitive arenas.

The diagrams in this work illustrate the relationships among the various conceptual components of Sun Tzu's system. These relationships define Sun Tzu's ideas better than any English or Chinese terms we might use. In describing these concepts we use a combination of military terms drawn from the English language and Chinese terms drawn from both Mandarin and Cantonese. However, the key is to focus on the role that the elements play in the overall system rather than what those terms commonly mean in either language. Sun Tzu intentionally used many terms, such as the concept of *tao* for example, differently than his contemporaries. This is why he spends so much time in his work defining terms, but he defines those terms in the context of a well developed system of ancient science and philosophy that few today understand.

The purpose of this work is to provide a framework for understanding that philosophy. For those that related to ideas graphically, as opposed to verbally, this framework in invaluable.

New in This Edition

This work has won critical recognition and book award recognition in its earlier editions so we want to retain as much of its original character as possible. So we are offering minimal changes to the work. The biggest change is to connect the chapters of this work to the more detailed articles in our *Sun Tzu's Art of War Playbook*. Much of Sun Tzu's work is situation specific. If you find yourself in a certain situation where you want to find out more about how to respond, the 234 articles of the Playbook provide the information you need.

In a few other cases, we have updated the text to use the terminology that we use today. For example, we describe the uniting philosophy as "mission" instead of the more generic word, "philosophy" that we use in the basic translation. We also refer to the phrase "listen, aim, move, claim" to encapsulate Sun Tzu's general system of improving a position through knowledge, foreseeing, movement, and positioning, which again are the words used in the basic translation.

Gary Gagliardi, 2014

✦ ✦ ✦

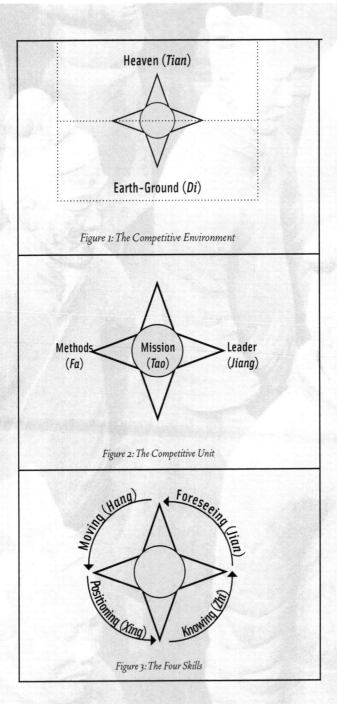

Heaven (*Tian*)

Earth-Ground (*Di*)

Figure 1: The Competitive Environment

Methods (*Fa*)   Mission (*Tao*)   Leader (*Jiang*)

Figure 2: The Competitive Unit

Moving (*Hang*)   Foreseeing (*Jian*)

Positioning (*Xing*)   Knowing (*Zhi*)

Figure 3: The Four Skills

Introduction

Sun Tzu's Strategic System

Without years of studying the original Chinese, most of the amazing sophistication of Sun Tzu's strategy is lost. Sun Tzu lived in a place and time with a wealth of cultural concepts that are alien to people today. Because of this, most readers today understand only a fraction of *The Art of War,* even those who read it in Chinese and especially those who read it in English translation. The purpose of this book is to explain the hidden secrets in the text. This work is based on many years of studying the original Chinese and teaching the its strategy worldwide.

Our explanation of the strategic science of the *Bing-Fa*—the Chinese name for what we call *The Art of War*—is offered in parallel with our award-winning English translation. *The Art of War* is shown on the left-hand pages. On the facing right-hand pages, the hidden secrets of each stanza are explained.

Using Sun Tzu's strategy, success goes not to the strongest or most aggressive but to those who best understand their situation and what their alternatives are. When you master Sun Tzu's strategic methods, you we can quickly see through the complexity of challenging situations to spot opportunities and make the right decisions. Strategy is less about winning battles than it is about winning without battle. Good strategists seek positions that are so powerful that no one challenges them. Fighting opponents openly is usually the failure of strategy.

Since competitive situations can seem almost overwhelmingly complex, Sun Tzu's work often refers back to the five simple concepts that he introduces in the first section of his first chapter. These five elements—mission (*tao*), heaven (*tian*), earth (*di*), the leader (*jiang*), and methods (*fa*)—provide the backbone of his competitive approach. All the other components of his system—deception (*gui*), completeness (*quan*), knowledge (*zhi*), fullness (*sat*), and so on—have very specific and practical relationships to these five elements. The depth and sophistication of his system is best understood if we spend a little time exploring the interrelationships of his key elements before discussing the text of his work.

The interrelationships among these five key components are critical to understanding them. To illustrate these relationships, we use *yao*—written in Chinese as 爻—diagrams, which were originally used for divination. The ancient Chinese traditionally used diagrams to describe the relationships of key elements in science and philosophy. The *I Ching*, feng shui, Chinese medicine, and classical Chinese physics are all based on specific *yao*. The *ba-gua*, the "flying-star," and the "elemental star-pentagram" are all surviving examples.

Diagramming predates Sun Tzu, making it likely that when he developed *bing-fa*, he used similar tools. Though we have no surviving examples of Sun Tzu's *yao*, we can recreate them from the text. We show these *yao* as illustrations at the beginning of every chapter to demonstrate the key relationships. The clarity with which they express Sun Tzu's principles is perhaps the most important secret hidden in the text and offered in this book.

Beginning with the five elements, Sun Tzu teaches that every competitive situation depends upon the unique relative position of a competitor within the larger competitive environment. As with so many of Sun Tzu's basic concepts, he describes the environment as two opposite and yet complementary halves: *tian,* which literally means "heaven," and *di,* the earth (*Figure 1, page 12*). The strategic position—the four-pointed star in the diagram—defines a specific position within this larger environment. Heaven and earth together represent the time and place in which competition occurs.

In one sense, *tian* or heaven represents the timing of competition, but more accurately it describes the general atmosphere of change, translated as "climate," or "weather" in English. We can think of "heaven" as trends that change over time. Weather and the cycle of the seasons are the most obvious aspects of a changing heaven in the physical battlefield. In the business environment, the business climate, economic trends, and business cycles carry close to the same meaning as Sun Tzu's *tian.*

Di or earth is both where we fight and what we fight over. It is the territory in which the competitive battle takes place. It is also the territory that provides economic support for a strategic position. In the business world, we can think of the earth as our job environment or the larger marketplace. Any competitive arena that generates income is a form of ground or earth. Unlike heaven, which is largely beyond our control, the most important aspect of the earth is that we control our position within it. Choosing positions on the earth, moving to them, and utilizing them are the main basis of Sun Tzu's strategy.

Within this larger competitive environment of heaven and earth, a strategic position is defined by five key factors (*Figure 2*). A competitor's specific time and place within the larger environment are an expression of the same concepts, *tian* and *di,* that describe the larger environment itself. Within a competitive unit, the climate or *tian* is determined by attitude and emotions, the changeable part of our natures. The term, *di,* means earth but it also means situation or condition. In Sun Tzu's system, the uniqueness of a competitor's position in time and space and the uniqueness of their attitude and condition, are key components of its strategic position. However, there are three other elements that make up a strategic position as well.

Jiang, the commander or general, is the person whose decisions direct the competitive contest. Leadership is the realm of individual action and character. A leader masters the skills or strategy so that he or she can make the right decisions quickly.

Fa, meaning "laws" or "methods," are the rules, organization, and systems that define an organization and its techniques for operation. Methods are the result of a leader's decisions. Though methods can be used by a single person, methods are, by definition, the realm of group action and interaction. Commanders make decisions as individuals, but it is the effect of those decisions upon the group that makes the organization effective. Strategy takes place only in the world of human competition.

Binding and underlying the other four components of a strategic position is *tao,* the mission as a uniting philosophy. *Tao* is the unique idea around which a specific strategic position is organized. In business, we call this a company mission or purpose. A core mission provides an individual competitor with oneness, unity, or completeness (*quan*), thereby joining its individual commander and methods with the larger group. The mission also provides the competitor's focus (*zhuan*) on a specific time and place. The shared goals of a mission holds the competitive organization together. This is why *tao* is shown as the center of the four-pointed star that illustrates a strategic position in Sun Tzu's system (*Figure 2*).

Understanding these five-elements describing a strategic position is the basis for understanding the rest of Sun Tzu's competitive concepts and methods.

For example, four different types of external skills are referenced again and again throughout the text. These skills are knowing (*zhi*), foreseeing (*jian*), moving (*hang*), and positioning (*xing*). The

Chinese concepts work both as verbs and nouns, so in the text we also refer to *zhi* as knowledge, *jian* as vision, *hang* as movement or action, and *xing* as position. However, these external skills are best understood by their relationship with the four external elements of strategic position (*Figure 3*). To make these concepts a little easier to remember, we also describe this cycle as the "listen, aim, move, claim cycle.

Individual leaders need the skills of knowing (listening) and foreseeing (aiming). Knowing or listening comes from the ground. Knowledge is the starting point for all other skills and the most critical component of strategy. It is covered extensively in the first chapter and the last. Knowing leads to foreseeing. Foreseeing or aiming is the vision of the leader seeing openings or opportunities in the future, which, in Sun Tzu's terms, means observing heaven—that is, the trends over time. Foreseeing is the ability to spot opportunities before others do.

The method skills of organizations are moving and positioning (claiming). Moving refers to taking any form of action, but it specifically means our ability to change positions to take advantage of a new opportunity. It comes from heaven or climate because movement requires proper timing and because emotion always precedes action. Movement arises from foresight (aim), and it leads naturally to positioning (claiming). *Xing,* the Chinese character used, literally means "form," but Sun Tzu gives the term the very specific meaning of claiming a ground position's advantages. You can be at a specific place, but you can't take advantage of that position unless you claim it. Controlling a positioning is the basis of all success.

In Sun Tzu's system, these four external skills create an endless cycle of progress. Knowing leads to foreseeing. Foreseeing necessitates moving. Moving gives us positioning. Positioning reinforces knowing. The leadership skills, knowing and foreseeing, are mental skills. The method skills, moving and positioning, are material skills. The cycle is also an economic one, with foreseeing and moving representing the cost part of the cycle and positioning and knowing the reward part of the cycle.

The four external skills are often referenced through metaphors. Knowing or listening is referred to as sound because knowing comes from listening. Thunder, music, and drums are all metaphors for knowing. Foresight or aiming is described as vision or seeing. Colors, lightning, and so on are metaphors for foresight. Moving is marching. Marching to a new position is the quintessential action. Positioning or claiming is variously described as gathering food, building, eating, digging, and so on. The commonality is that in the Chinese, these all use pictographs involving the human hand, so generally, handiwork.

Sun Tzu also describes two other key abilities as internal skills: *quan* and *zhuan*. *Quan* means literally "complete," or "oneness" but Sun Tzu uses it to mean "united." *Zhuan* means "to concentrate on," or what we would describe as focus. Though these concepts are separate in English, in classical strategy they are two sides of the same coin. Both arise directly from our mission as a uniting philosophy, and its relationship with the leader and his or her methods. Completeness unites and holds the organization together (*Figure 4, page 21*). Focus or single-mindeness concentrates efforts in a single place and time (*Figure 5*). These two internal skills of unity and focus arise from mission, which is the foundation of strategy.

Notice that none of these skills, either internal or external, focus on beating opponents or engaging in conflict (*zheng*). Instead, the strategy of *bing-fa* makes competitive progress by continually improving and advancing our strategic position. Faced with challenging a strong strategic position, opponents surrender without conflict.

Though *bing-fa* shows us how to find success in competitive situations, Sun Tzu's recipe for success is to avoid unnecessary conflict. He sees such conflict as inherently costly. He teaches us how to handle direct, hostile confrontations when they cannot be avoided, but his basic approach is to defuse these situations before they occur. His method is psychological: we must convince potential opponents to give us what we want without a fight. We must convince the people on our team to present a united front so that others will not challenge us. Sun Tzu taught the art of persuasion and team building as an alternative to destructive confrontations in competitive situations.

Sun Tzu teaches that there are five ways our progress can be disrupted by opponents or, conversely, we can hamper their progress. Four of these disruptions—deception (*gui*), division (*fen*), battle (*zhan*), innovation (*qi jang*), and siege (*gong cheng*)—are aimed specifically at the external skills that allow progress (*Figure 6*). *Gui* is the bluffing, deception, or illusions that spoil foresight and aim. *Zhan* is translated as "battles" but literally means meeting an opponent to counter their movement but not necessarily conflict. Battle is always used with innovation—*qi jang*—which undermines knowledge. *Gong cheng* (literally "strike cities") lays siege to a position. The fifth form of disruption, divide (*fen*) is aimed at unity and focus, breaking apart a share mission.

It is best to think of these concepts in terms of the relationships that they have with other system components. Strategy sees a competitive situation as a dynamic whole in which all the parts continually interact and change. Because of this, the graphical relationships often define the nature of these concepts better than the terms that we use. A good example is the case of what we call "deception," which means hampering another's vision through the use of illusion or bluffing.

One of the keys to successful strategy is picking the right battleground—that is, selecting the right focus for our activities. Everyone has limited resources. In making decisions, we must evaluate what can be done and what can be left undone, picking the best possible places to invest our limited resources, especially the resource of time.

Sun Tzu offers a cooperative view of competition. According to his teaching, we cannot succeed through our own actions alone. We don't create opportunities. We can defend our existing position from attack, but the competitive environment itself generates opportunities for our success. The secret is recognizing these opportunities when they present themselves, and, once we recognize them, we must have the confidence to act. Since every problem creates an opportunity, strategy teaches that opportunities are abundant but difficult to recognize and act upon.

Finally, Sun Tzu's strategic system is knowledge-intensive. Sun Tzu sees success going to the best-informed and best-educated decision-makers. This is why we consider knowledge the beginning point for all competitive progress. There is no substitute for good information. It is worth any price. *The Art of War's* last chapter, USING SPIES, explains all the types of information we must acquire.

Despite its relatively short length, this book contains a wealth of detail about how strategy works. Do not expect to appreciate all of its principles in one reading. You should also consider acquiring our other books on mastering strategy to help you flesh out your understanding of how to succeed in an increasingly competitive world. Time spent studying Sun Tzu's system is always time well invested.

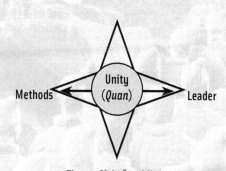

Figure 4: Unity from Mission

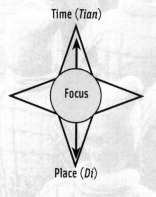

Figure 5: Focus from Mission

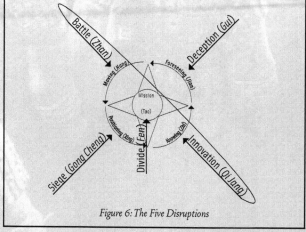

Figure 6: The Five Disruptions

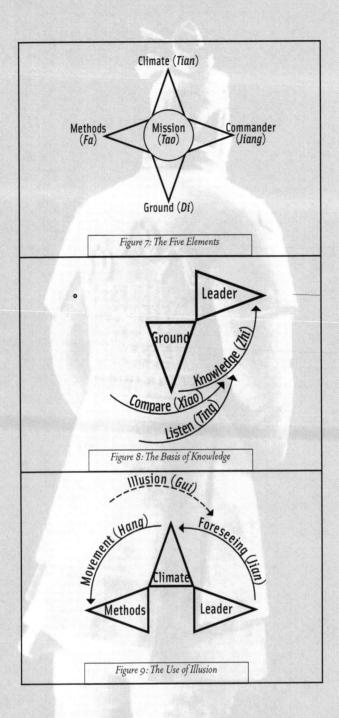

Climate (*Tian*)

Methods
(*Fa*)   Mission
(*Tao*)   Commander
(*Jiang*)

Ground (*Di*)

Figure 7: The Five Elements

Leader

Ground

Knowledge (*Zhi*)

Compare (*Xiao*)

Listen (*Ting*)

Figure 8: The Basis of Knowledge

Illusion (*Gui*)

Movement (*Hang*)

Foreseeing (*Jian*)

Climate

Methods   Leader

Figure 9: The Use of Illusion

Chapter 1

Analysis

Although Sun Tzu named his first chapter 計 in Chinese, which translates to "plan" or "planning" in English, his meaning is much closer to what we would call competitive analysis.

In the chapter's first section, Sun Tzu describes the major components that make up competitive systems, but throughout the book, the interrelationships between components are as important as the components themselves. The base diagram, the *Five-Element Star* (*Figure 7*) shows the basic relationships among the five factors used in *bing-fa* for analyzing competitive systems.

In the *Star*, the core is *tao*, the mission as a uniting philosophy that unites a competitive unit and focuses it on its position. The four arms of the *Star* are the other major components introduced in this chapter: the leader (*jiang*), the climate (*tian*), the methods (*fa*), and the ground (*di*).

The next major topic of this chapter is knowledge (*zhi*). Knowledge (*Figure 8*) comes from the ground or situation (*di*) and passes to the leader (*jiang*). Knowledge is supported by comparison (*xiao*) and listening (*ting*).

The chapter's final major topic (*Figure 9*) is deception or illusion (*gui*), which means creating a false appearance. Appearance is the realm of vision (*jian*), which is the basis of action or movement (*hang*). By providing false vision, that is, an illusion, we can be misled and which we use to mislead our opponents.

Analysis

SUN TZU SAID:

This is war. 1

It is the most important skill in the nation.

It is the basis of life and death.

It is the philosophy of survival or destruction.

You must know it well.

⁶Your skill comes from five factors.

Study these factors when you plan war.

You must insist on knowing your situation.

1.	Discuss philosophy.
2.	Discuss the climate.
3.	Discuss the ground.
4.	Discuss leadership.
5.	Discuss military methods.

¹⁴It starts with your military philosophy.

Command your people in a way that gives them a higher shared purpose.

You can lead them to death.

You can lead them to life.

They must never fear danger or dishonesty.

Competitive Systems

1 The topic is war, but more broadly it is how competitive systems work. In many ways, Sun Tzu's work anticipated Darwin in seeing that competition is a matter of survival, and that survival depends upon having specific skills, but for human competition Sun Tzu teaches that these skills can be learned.

Like Darwin, Sun Tzu also taught that success in war depends on our relationship with the larger environment. He defines that position by five concepts. The Chinese terms for these are:
1. *Tao*: literally "way," the mission that acts as a uniting force
2. *Tian*: literally "heaven," meaning the trends in time
3. *Di*: the "ground" on which we compete
4. *Jiang*: the "general," but meaning the leader or decision-maker
5. *Fa*: our "methods," which include our procedures and systems

The most important component in this model is the Chinese concept of *tao*, which is means "way" and is translated as "philosophy." Sun Tzu defines it specifically as the uniting mission of an organization. Our mission must be people-centered, giving people a way to meet their goals and a higher purpose. It must hold the organization together as the source of focus and unity.

[19]Next, you have the climate.
It can be sunny or overcast.
It can be hot or cold.
It includes the timing of the seasons.

[23]Next is the terrain.
It can be distant or near.
It can be difficult or easy.
It can be open or narrow.
It also determines your life or death.

[28]Next is the commander.
He must be smart, trustworthy, caring, brave, and strict.

[30]Finally, you have your military methods.
They include the shape of your organization.
This comes from your management philosophy.
You must master their use.

[34]All five of these factors are critical.
As a commander, you must pay attention to them.
Understanding them brings victory.
Ignoring them means defeat.

Though translated as "climate," the original Chinese character is *tian*, which means "sky" or "heaven." This is the part of the environment that is beyond our control and changes constantly with time. Like the seasons, we can look for patterns of change.

The terrain or ground, *di* in Chinese, is both where we fight and what we fight over. However, *di* also means condition and situation—that is, how we are placed or situated. The ground is literally the source of life and all income. Its characteristics both as physical ground and as types of situations are a major topic of *bing-fa*.

The leader (or *jiang*, for "general") creates and defines the competitive unit by his character and decision-making skills.

Our systems, organizations, processes, and procedures are all part of our methods, or the Chinese concept of *fa*. Methods must be efficient and effective, but they must also be consistent with our central organizing purpose or *tao*.

These five key elements are extensively discussed and defined in the course of the book. Each chapter focuses on one or more of these elements. Sun Tzu taught that our success is determined by how well we master these elements.

You must learn through planning. 2
You must question the situation.

3You must ask:
Which government has the right philosophy?
Which commander has the skill?
Which season and place has the advantage?
Which method of command works?
Which group of forces has the strength?
Which officers and men have the training?
Which rewards and punishments make sense?
This tells when you will win and when you will lose.
Some commanders perform this analysis.
If you use these commanders, you will win.
Keep them.
Some commanders ignore this analysis.
If you use these commanders, you will lose.
Get rid of them.

Plan an advantage by listening. 3
Adjust to the situations.
Get assistance from the outside.
Influence events.
Then planning can find opportunities and give you control.

2 The concept is *xiao*, which is translated as "learn," but it also means "compare" or "proofread," in the sense of "double check."

Bing-fa teaches us to double check our facts when we compare ourselves with our opponents. We can never say how "good" anything is without comparing it to existing alternatives—in this case, our opponents. Our competitive decisions are made based on comparing our situation and abilities with those of our opponents. The five factors provide the basis for this comparative analysis. We must constantly compare our mission (*tao*), our timing (*tian*), our ground (*di*), our management abilities (*jiang*), and our procedures (*fa*) with those of our opponents. This comparative analysis allows us to match our strengths against an opponent's weaknesses. This alone lets us prioritize an infinite number of possible actions. To be successful leaders, we must insist on working with people who understand how to evaluate their relative position or power. Sun Tzu attributes most failure to decision-making by people who refuse to do the necessary comparisons.

3 The foundation of competitive analysis is knowledge (*zhi*), but the base of knowledge is *ting*, listening or heeding others, especially from outside viewpoints. We must continually open ourselves to new ideas that come in from outside our normal channels of information. This new information is the source of *li*, opportunity.

Warfare is one thing. 4
It is a philosophy of deception.

3When you are ready, you try to appear incapacitated.
When active, you pretend inactivity.
When you are close to the enemy, you appear distant.
When far away, you pretend you are near.

7If the enemy has a strong position, entice him away from it.
If the enemy is confused, be decisive.
If the enemy is solid, prepare against him.
If the enemy is strong, avoid him.
If the enemy is angry, frustrate him.
If the enemy is weaker, make him arrogant.
If the enemy is relaxed, make him work.
If the enemy is united, break him apart.
Attack him when he is unprepared.
Leave when he least expects it.

17You will find a place where you can win.
You cannot first signal your intentions.

4 The Chinese term *gui* is translated as "deception," but it doesn't mean dishonesty. Its meaning is closer to "illusion."

In competition, ignorance is safer than the illusion of knowledge. Illusion is an attack on vision (*jian*), creating a false appearance. Keeping competitors ignorant is good; it stops them from acting. Vision leads to movement (*hang*), so illusion leads to mistakes.

Illusion (*gui*) has a host of uses since it controls people's perceptions. Vision leads to actions because it is based on emotion as much as fact. We use appearance to influence other people's emotions because emotions are the trigger for action. We tailor our actions to incite people's emotions enough to motivate them into action. In misleading opponents, we cause them to waste their efforts. Once we can get people moving, they are more easily guided and predicted. Though this section is about working on the emotions of opponents, these methods work equally well in motivating the people with whom we work.

We use *gui* to put ourselves into a position where people will do what we desire. When we win this credibility, we must use it.

Manage to avoid battle until your organization can count on certain victory.

You must calculate many advantages.

Before you go to battle, your organization's analysis can indicate that you may not win.

You can count few advantages.

Many advantages add up to victory.

Few advantages add up to defeat.

How can you know your advantages without analyzing them?

We can see where we are by means of our observations.

We can foresee our victory or defeat by planning.

♦ ♦ ♦

5 Success in competition depends on our vision, that is, our ability to foresee our relative strength at a specific time and place. *Bing-fa* teaches that, given an honest evaluation of our strengths and weaknesses, we can foresee when and where we will be successful. Sun Tzu saw this analysis as a simple mathematical comparison, which is covered in more detail in chapter 4. The mistake that most people make is considering only their own abilities without considering how these abilities compare with those of the competition. All ability is relative. We have a choice about where and when we compete. We must choose to compete only where and when we can beat any possible competition.

Related Articles from *Sun Tzu's Playbook*

In this first chapter, Sun Tzu introduces the basics of positioning. We explore these ideas in more detail in our Sun Tzu's Art of War Playbook. To learn the step-by-step techniques for positioning, we recommend the Playbook articles listed below.

1.0.0 Strategic Positioning: developing relatively superior positions.

1.1.0 Position Paths: the continuity of strategic positions over time.

1.1.1 Position Dynamics: how all current positions evolve over time.

1.1.2 Defending Positions: defending current positions until new positions are established.

1.2 Subobjective Positions: the subjective and objective aspects of a position.

1.2.1 Competitive Landscapes: the arenas in which rivals jockey for position.

1.2.2 Exploiting Exploration: how competitive landscapes are searched and positions identified.

1.2.3 Position Complexity: how positions arise from interactions in complex environments.

1.3 Elemental Analysis: the relevant components of all competitive positions.

1.3.1 Competitive Comparison: competition as the comparison of positions.

1.3.2 Element Scalability: how elements of a position scale up to larger positions.

1.4 The External Environment: external conditions shaping strategic positions.

1.4.1 Climate Shift: forces of environmental change shaping temporary conditions.

1.4.2 Ground Features: the persistent resources that we can control.

1.5 Competing Agents: the key characteristics of competitors.

1.5.1 Command Leadership: individual decision-making.

1.5.2. Group Methods: systems for executing decisions.

1.6 Mission Values: the goals and values needed for motivation.

1.6.1 Shared Mission: finding goals that others can share.

1.6.2 Types of Motivations: hierarchies of motivation that define missions.

1.6.3 Shifting Priorities: how missions change according to temporary conditions.

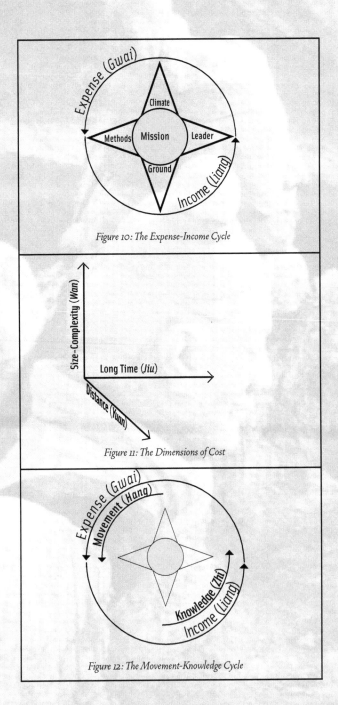

Figure 10: The Expense-Income Cycle

Figure 11: The Dimensions of Cost

Figure 12: The Movement-Knowledge Cycle

Chapter 2

作戰

Going to War: Competitive Economics

In Chinese, this chapter's title is "make battle" where battle (*zhan*) means meeting an enemy or a challenge. In it, Sun Tzu looks at the economics of war. He does not define victory as beating opponents. He defines success as making victory pay. This economic focus is why this strategy works so well in today's business world.

In strategy, the cycle of expense and income can be diagrammed (*Figure 10*) using the five-element star introduced in the last chapter. Expenses belong to the realm of heaven or climate, which means that they are associated with time and the cost of resources are beyond our control. Most of this chapter deals with the expense side of this equation. Income or provisions, in contrast, come from the ground, that is, positions that we can control.

Sun Tzu describes three dimensions that increase costs (*Figure 11*). Costs aren't only expenses but time and our probability of success as well. The first dimension is called "size," but the Chinese concept *wan* means literally "myriad" or "ten thousand," implying complexity as well as size. The next dimension is time, *jiu*, which means a "long time" and suggests delay. The final dimension is distance, *yuan*, which is used in all cost calculations.

Movement is a physical act and is associated with increasing cost, but its opposite, knowledge, is a mental ability and is just as strongly associated with reducing costs or generating income (*Figure 12*).

Going to War

Everything depends on your use of military philosophy. 1
Moving the army requires thousands of vehicles.
These vehicles must be loaded thousands of times.
The army must carry a huge supply of arms.
You need ten thousand acres of grain.
This results in internal and external shortages.
Any army consumes resources like an invader.
It uses up glue and paint for wood.
It requires armor for its vehicles.
People complain about the waste of a vast amount of metal.
It will set you back when you attempt to raise tens of thousands of troops.

¹²Using a huge army makes war very expensive to win.
Long delays create a dull army and sharp defeats.
Attacking enemy cities drains your forces.
Long violent campaigns that exhaust the nation's resources are wrong.

Competitive Economics

1 This chapter is a critical discussion of the economics of competitive action. Sun Tzu views all competitive missions as inherently economic. Competitive efforts consume resources more intensively than productive efforts—represented in *bing-fa* by civilian society—with much less predictable results. Competitive efforts require moving resources to new positions. Movement requires costly transportation. In competition, we need enough resources to survive. Since all resources are inherently limited, competitive efforts steal time, energy, and money away from productive activities. Since many competitive efforts fail, these resources are often lost. The most limited resource required by strategic competition is our investment of time.

Sun Tzu's view of competition is often mathematical. The cost of a competitive effort is determined by the size of that effort multiplied by its duration. Striking at an enemy's strong points and confrontation in general, requires huge investments. This expense is why his strategy is fundamentally opposed to direct confrontation.

¹⁶Manage a dull army.

You will suffer sharp defeats.

You will drain your forces.

Your money will be used up.

Your rivals will multiply as your army collapses and they will begin against you.

It doesn't matter how smart you are.

You cannot get ahead by taking losses!

²³You hear of people going to war too quickly.

Still, you won't see a skilled war that lasts a long time.

²⁵You can fight a war for a long time or you can make your nation strong.

You can't do both.

Make no assumptions about all the dangers in using military force. **2**

Then you won't make assumptions about the benefits of using arms either.

³You want to make good use of war.

Do not raise troops repeatedly.

Do not carry too many supplies.

Choose to be useful to your nation.

Feed off the enemy.

Make your army carry only the provisions it needs.

Sun Tzu teaches that economic miscalculations cascade into bigger and bigger problems. The problem isn't simply taking risks and failing. We can't afford to make large, costly mistakes because we cannot recover from them. In competition, we survive only as long as we have the resources to continue. When we have resources, we have friends. When we lack resources, the world turns its back on us. Our first priority in competitive action is to preserve our financial strength. We can never afford to spend our way to success.

Competitive campaigns must be short, with the immediate goal of getting to a point where they can generate revenue or rewards.

If we quickly get to the point where a competitive action generates revenue instead of consuming it, competitive action increases our opportunities instead of decreasing them. Costly time is our enemy.

2 Competition is the realm of chaos. Competitive efforts do not have predictable results in the same way that productive efforts do. Competition can bring us much more or much less success than we expect. We cannot know without trying, but we must take care.

Good strategy teaches us to be very financially conservative. We must limit our spending. We must do our tasks correctly the first time. We cannot afford to redo them. We can never afford to be extravagant. The less we spend on a competitive effort, the more quickly our efforts can become profitable and start generating resources instead of consuming them.

The nation impoverishes itself shipping to troops that 3 are far away.

Distant transportation is costly for hundreds of families.

Buying goods with the army nearby is also expensive.

High prices also exhaust wealth.

If you exhaust your wealth, you then quickly hollow out your military.

Military forces consume a nation's wealth entirely.

War leaves households in the former heart of the nation with nothing.

[8]War destroys hundreds of families.

Out of every ten families, war leaves only seven.

War empties the government's storehouses.

Broken armies will get rid of their horses.

They will throw down their armor, helmets, and arrows.

They will lose their swords and shields.

They will leave their wagons without oxen.

War will consume 60 percent of everything you have.

Because of this, it is the intelligent commander's duty to 4 feed off the enemy.

[2]Use a cup of the enemy's food.

It is worth twenty of your own.

Win a bushel of the enemy's feed.

It is worth twenty of your own.

3 Here Sun Tzu adds a third cost aspect to size and time, the dimension of distance. Distance means that we not only have to gather and distribute resources but that we have the additional cost of moving those resources as well. The dynamic nature of competitive positioning changes the natural, local balance of supply and demand, moving resources physically distant from their productive sources. The greater the physical space in which we try to compete, the more costly all our efforts must be. We must avoid action over a distance and protect ourselves against getting sucked into investing more and more into more and more distant arenas.

Competition is difficult and painful. Most competitors are unsuccessful most of the time. Eighty percent of new businesses fail within their first two years. Their losses usually are complete. People lose their entire life savings. All the care, effort, and value that people try to build up in creating their success can be easily lost. In competition, simply putting in the time and effort does not guarantee results, and when things go wrong, people are extremely likely to panic and throw away everything they have.

4 The cost of competition means that we must generate resources from our efforts rather than just consuming them.

A dollar is not always a dollar. Resources that we win from the competition are worth twenty times more than resources that we already own because they represent competitive progress. Progress is the food that feeds our future competitive success.

⁶You can kill the enemy and frustrate him as well.
Take the enemy's strength from him by stealing away his
money.

⁸Fight for the enemy's supply wagons.
Capture his supplies by using overwhelming force.
Reward the first who capture them.
Then change their banners and flags.
Mix them in with your own wagons to increase your supply
line.
Keep your soldiers strong by providing for them.
This is what it means to beat the enemy while you grow
more powerful.

Make victory in war pay for itself. 5
Avoid expensive, long campaigns.
The military commander's knowledge is the key.
It determines if the civilian officials can govern.
It determines if the nation's households are peaceful or a
danger to the state.

Our progress weakens our opponents' positions while it strengthens our own. The text focuses everywhere else on economic resources in general, but here the issue specifically becomes money.

Sun Tzu teaches that the most meaningful success is taking resources away from our opponents. We must always focus our efforts on obtaining resources. Since rewarding people requires resources, the primary people that we want to reward should be those who obtain resources. We identify these newly won resources as our own and utilize them rather than hold them hostage or as a trophy. We must reinvest these resources in our competitive progress. The more resources we have, the more we can do. The more resources we control, the weaker our competition becomes.

5 Sun Tzu teaches that the secret to success is simply making our competitive progress pay for itself. The first key to winning the economic battle is keeping our costs low. We must always remember this when we make decisions. The civilian or productive part of our efforts cannot be successful if our competitive efforts consume all our resources.

Related Articles from *Sun Tzu's Playbook*

In his second chapter, Sun Tzu teaches basic competitive economics. We explore these ideas in more detail in our **Sun Tzu's Art of War Playbook**. *To learn the step-by-step techniques for economical political campaigning, we recommend the articles listed below.*

1.3.1 Competitive Comparison: competition as the comparison of positions.

1.6.1 Shared Mission: finding goals that others can share.

1.8.3 Cycle Time: speed in feedback and reaction.

1.8.4 Probabilistic Process: the role of chance in strategic processes and systems.

2.2.1 Personal Relationships: how information depends on personal relationships.

2.2.2 Mental Models: how mental models simplify decision-making.

2.3.4 Using Questions: using questions in gathering information and predicting reactions.

3.1 Strategic Economics: balancing the cost and benefits of positioning.

3.1.1 Resource Limitations: the inherent limitation of strategic resources.

3.1.2 Strategic Profitability: understanding gains and losses.

3.1.3 Conflict Cost: the costly nature of resolving competitive comparisons by conflict.

3.1.4 Openings: seeking openings to avoid costly conflict.

3.1.5 Unpredictable Value: the limitations of predicting the value of positions.

3.1.6 Time Limitations: the time limits on opportunities.

4.0 Leveraging Probability: better decisions regarding our choice of opportunities.

4.1 Future Potential: the limitations and potential of current and future positions.

4.2 Choosing Non-Action: choosing between action and non-action.

5.3 Reaction Time: the use of speed in choosing actions.

5.3.1 Speed and Quickness: the use of pace within a dynamic environment.

5.3.2 Opportunity Windows: the effect of speed upon opposition.

5.3.3 Information Freshness: choosing actions based on freshness of information.

5.4 Minimizing Action: minimizing waste, i.e., less is more.

5.4.1 Testing Value : choosing actions to test for value.

5.4.2 Successful Mistakes: learning from our mistakes.

5.5 Focused Power: size consideration in safe experimentation.

5.5.1 Force Size: limiting the size of force in an advance.

5.5.2 Distance Limitations: the use of short steps to reach distant goals.

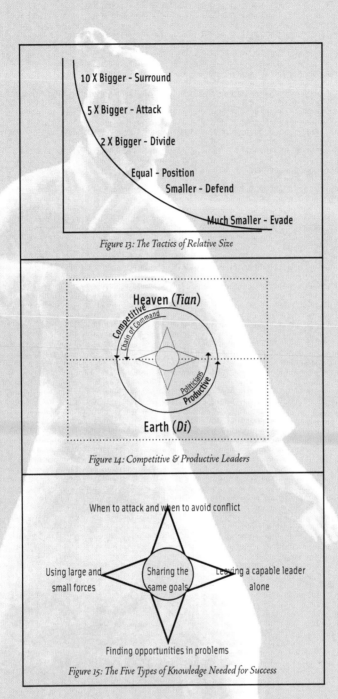

10 X Bigger - Surround

5 X Bigger - Attack

2 X Bigger - Divide

Equal - Position
Smaller - Defend

Much Smaller - Evade

Figure 13: The Tactics of Relative Size

Heaven (*Tian*)

Competitive
Chain of Command

Politicians
Productive

Earth (*Di*)

Figure 14: Competitive & Productive Leaders

When to attack and when to avoid conflict

Using large and
small forces

Sharing the
same goals

Leaving a capable leader
alone

Finding opportunities in problems

Figure 15: The Five Types of Knowledge Needed for Success

Chapter 3

Planning an Attack

The central topic of this chapter is unity, focus, and speed and their effect on the relative strength of an organization.

In the chapter's first section, Sun Tzu says that unity and focus (*see Figures 4 and 5 on page 21*) are required at every level of an organization. The goal of unity and focus is not to win conflict but to succeed without conflict.

Sun Tzu then lists the basic forms of attack (*see Figure 6, page 21* in descending order of importance. The text then warns against the worst of these: laying siege to another's strong position.

In the third section, Sun Tzu suggests an incremental approach to success: using small, focused engagement where we have the clear advantage. He lists our tactics based on relative size (*Figure 13*).

In section four, we are warned against political divisions within an organization. In *classical strategy*, a natural division occurs between an organization's productive half, the nation, and its competitive force, the army (*Figure 14*). These two halves must support one another, and the politicians controlling the nation must let commanders control the competitive forces.

Sun Tzu then details the five areas of knowledge that determine our ability to unite and concentrate our forces. These five areas diagram against the five key elements in competition (*Figure 15*).

He ends with a warning about the dangers of miscalculating the relative strength our organization is facing in competition.

Planning an Attack

SUN TZU SAID:

Everyone relies on the arts of war. 1
A united nation is strong.
A divided nation is weak.
A united army is strong.
A divided army is weak.
A united force is strong.
A divided force is weak.
United men are strong.
Divided men are weak.
A united unit is strong.
A divided unit is weak.

[12]Unity works because it enables you to win every battle you
fight.
Still, this is the foolish goal of a weak leader.
Avoid battle and make the enemy's men surrender.
This is the right goal for a superior leader.

The best way to make war is to ruin the enemy's plans. 2
The next best is to disrupt alliances.
The next best is to attack the opposing army.
The worst is to attack the enemy's cities.

Unity, Focus, and Speed

1 The primary requirement of a competitive attack or campaign is unity and focus. In classical strategy, these come from our mission, the shared philosophy that brings people together. We translate the Chinese term *muo* as "united," but its literal meaning is closer to "complete" or "whole." Its opposing concept, *po*, translated as "divided," means literally "broken" or "worn out." Sun Tzu teaches that the cohesion within an organization is the source of strength in competition. Any organization is strong only when it has a core of strongly shared values, or *tao*. However, the cohesion of any larger organization is only as good as the cohesion of its various parts, each with its own unique purpose or function.

The next issue in a competitive campaign is its goal. Again, in classical strategy, the goal is never to confront opponents. Beating opponents is a childish view of competitive success. The goal should be to develop a competitive position that is so powerful that no one challenges us. This is the central purpose of strategy.

2 Sun Tzu prioritizes the forms of attack. The best is destroying plans using *gui*, that is, misdirection attacking vision. Next is using our power to divide, breaking organizations. Worse is battle, moving against opponents. The worst is attacking solid positions.

5This is what happens when you attack a city.
You can attempt it, but you can't finish it.
First you must make siege engines.
You need the right equipment and machinery.
It takes three months and still you cannot win.
Then you try to encircle the area.
You use three more months without making progress.
Your command still doesn't succeed and this angers you.
You then try to swarm the city.
This kills a third of your officers and men.
You are still unable to draw the enemy out of the city.
This attack is a disaster.

Make good use of war. 3
Make the enemy's troops surrender.
You can do this fighting only minor battles.
You can draw their men out of their cities.
You can do it with small attacks.
You can destroy the men of a nation.
You must keep your campaign short.

8You must use total war, fighting with everything you have.
Never stop fighting when at war.
You can gain complete advantage.
To do this, you must plan your strategy of attack.

Sun Tzu's strategy teaches us to avoid attempts to destroy opposing positions. An opponent's successful, established positions are obvious targets and seemingly desirable prizes, but this makes them expensive targets, leading to costly wars of attrition that no one wins. The power that makes a taken position desirable also makes it unattainable. We must remember the lessons of the last chapter about limiting our expenditures of time and resources. Trying to win an opponent's established position is always the most costly form of advancing our position, in both time and effort. And, no matter how many resources we put into such an attack, it is unlikely to ever succeed. We must fight against our natural desire for such positions and not challenge them directly.

3 When we are planning a competitive move, we seek positions where others cannot resist us. We seek ways to win them in quick, small, and local contests. We can draw our opponents away from their strong points to compete on our terms. We plan incremental actions that ruin opponents' plans, break up their organizations, and inhibit their movement. These moves drain away opponents' resources and will to fight. Acting quickly keeps them off balance.

We must put our efforts into these quick campaigns, and one campaign must immediately follow the other. Our ultimate advantage comes from a series of quick victories that discourage opponents. This requires carefully choosing the right opportunities.

[12]The rules for making war are:
If you outnumber enemy forces ten to one, surround them.
If you outnumber them five to one, attack them.
If you outnumber them two to one, divide them.
If you are equal, then find an advantageous battle.
If you are fewer, defend against them.
If you are much weaker, evade them.

[19]Small forces are not powerful.
However, large forces cannot catch them.

You must master command. 4
The nation must support you.

[3]Supporting the military makes the nation powerful.
Not supporting the military makes the nation weak.

[5]The army's position is made more difficult by politicians in
three different ways.
Ignorant of a military division's inability to advance, they
order an advance.
Ignorant of a military division's inability to withdraw, they
order a withdrawal.
We call this tying up the army.
They don't understands a military division's function.
Still, they think they can govern military divisions.
This confuses the army's officers.

Sun Tzu teaches that overall size is not the source of strength. Force (*shi*) comes from our ability to concentrate our resources at the specific place and time. Our tactics during a contest depend entirely upon the local, relative balance of power. Ideally, we completely outnumber our opposition. When this is not possible, we act according to our relative strength: we divide our opponents, pick our battles, defend our strong points, or avoid contact entirely.

Size is both an advantage and a disadvantage. Large groups can overpower small ones, but small groups can move more quickly.

4 Think of "the nation" (*guo*) as the internal organization, producing goods and services, less involved in external competition.

Only competitive success gives us an outlet for our productive efforts. Without such success, our production skills are wasted.

Sun Tzu's strategy recognizes that inherent differences divide the competitive and the productive parts of any organization. Productivity requires long-term planning and control. Competitive action requires intimate knowledge of the immediate situation and quick adaptability. Competitive moves cannot be made based upon the internal desires of the productive organization. Competitive moves much be made when the situation is right. Decision-makers from productive parts of the organization seldom appreciate how dependent competitive success is upon the dynamics of the larger environment. Remote decision-making doesn't work in competition.

¹²Politicians don't know the military division of authority.
They think all military divisions are the same.
This will create distrust among the army's officers.

¹⁵Military divisions can become confused and suspicious.
This invites invasion by many different rivals.
We say correctly that disorder in an army kills victory.

You must know five things to win: 5
Victory comes from knowing when to attack and when to
avoid battle.
Victory comes from correctly using both large and small
forces.
Victory comes from everyone sharing the same goals.
Victory comes from finding opportunities in problems.
Victory comes from having a capable commander and the
government leaving him alone.
You must know these five things.
You then know the theory of victory.

We say: 6
"Know yourself and know your enemy.
You will be safe in every battle.
You may know yourself but not know the enemy.
You will then lose one battle for every one you win.
You may not know yourself or the enemy.
You will then lose every battle."

Managers also fail to appreciate the division of responsibility in competition. Every competitive situation is unique. Those on the front-lines must trust their organization to trust them.

Those on the front-line can become confused about their authority and mission. Opponents sense their competitive uncertainty. This confusion destroy the possibility of competitive success.

5 The fives types of knowledge required in competition map into the five key elements introduced in the first chapter. Knowing when to meet opponents and, just as importantly, when not to meet them, is based on *tian*, the current trends. Knowing how to use different sized forces is a matter of *fa*, understanding methods. Sharing the same goals requires *tao*, an underlying, uniting mission. Discovering opportunities demands knowledge of *di*, the competitive ground. Finally, the organization needs to know who the ultimate decision maker is, the *jiang*, the general and competitive leader. The effects of unity, focus, and speed can only be evaluated within the complete context of our competitive situation.

6 It isn't enough simply to know what we can do in a competitive situation. We must also understand what our opponents can do in response. Our first goal in developing this knowledge is our safety: preserving our ability to compete. Our information is never perfect, but there is a direct mathematical relationship between how much we know and how successful we are. The more we know about our relative positions, the more successful we will be.

♦ ♦ ♦

Related Articles from *Sun Tzu's Playbook*

In this third chapter, Sun Tzu introduces the basics of advancing into new areas. To learn the step-by-step techniques involved, we recommend the Sun Tzu's Art of War Playbook *articles listed below.*

1.1.1 Position Dynamics: how all current positions are always getting better or worse.

1.1.2 Defending Positions: how we defend our current positions until new positions are established.

1.2 Subobjective Positions: the subjective and objective aspects of a position.

1.3.1 Competitive Comparison: competition as the comparison of positions.

1.7 Competitive Power: the sources of superiority in challenges.

1.7.1 Team Unity: strength by joining with others.

1.7.2 Goal Focus: strength as arising from concentrating efforts.

1.8 Progress Cycle: the adaptive loop by which positions are advanced.

1.8.1 Creation and Destruction: the creation and destruction of competitive positions.

1.8.2 The Adaptive Loop: the continual reiteration of position analysis.

2.3.6 Promises and Threats: the use of promises and threats as strategic moves.

2.4 Contact Networks: the range of contacts needed to create perspective.

2.4.1 Ground Perspective: getting information on a new competitive arena.

2.4.2 Climate Perspective: getting perspective on temporary external conditions.

3.0.0 Identifying Opportunities: the use of opportunities to advance a position.

3.1.3 Conflict Cost: the costly nature of resolving competitive comparisons by conflict.

3.2 Opportunity Creation: how change creates opportunities.

3.2.2 Opportunity Invisibility: why opportunities are always hidden.

3.2.4 Emptiness and Fullness: the transformations between strength and weakness.

3.4 Dis-Economies of Scale: how opportunities are created by the size of others.

3.4.2 Opportunity Fit: finding new opportunities that fit your size.

3.4.3 Reaction Lag: how size creates temporary openings.

3.5 Strength and Weakness: openings created by the strength of others.

3.6 Leveraging Subjectivity: openings between subjective and objective positions.

3.7 Defining the Ground: redefining a competitive arena to create relative mismatches.

5.6 Defensive Advances: balancing defending and advancing positions.

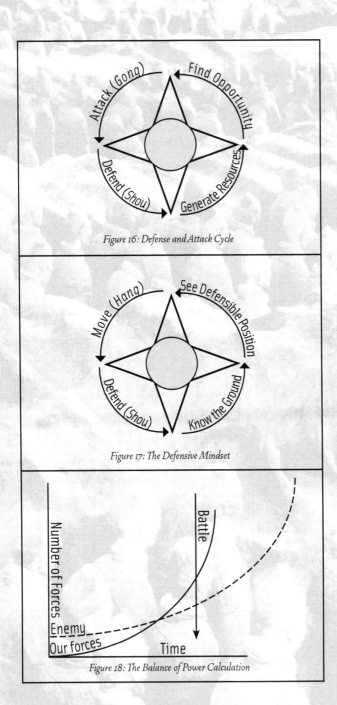

Figure 16: Defense and Attack Cycle

Figure 17: The Defensive Mindset

Figure 18: The Balance of Power Calculation

Chapter 4

Positioning: Awaiting Opportunities

The Chinese term *xing*, translated as "positioning," literally means "form." Sun Tzu uses it to mean the formation or concentration of resources at a position. We also call this claiming a position. A concentration can be defensive or offensive. An offensive move to a new position should only be made when a clear, certain-to-be-successful opportunity presents itself.

Sun Tzu starts by explaining the defense and attack cycle (*Figure 16*). An "attack" is any move to a new position. We can do no more than protect our existing position until the competitive environment creates an opportunity for a move. Our success initially depends on our ability to defend and generate surplus resources until an opportunity to move to a better position presents itself.

When we see an opportunity to move, we must still think about defense, asking ourselves how defensible our new position will be (*Figure 17*). After we see a defensible opportunity (foresight or aim), we must be able to both move to that new position and defend it when we get there.

Sun Tzu provides a simple formula for calculating whether or not we can succeed in winning a new position (*Figure 18*). This formula calculates the number of forces we can move to a specific place in a specific amount of time versus the amount of resources that our opponents can move to that position in a specific amount of time. This calculation is the foundation of positioning, *xing*, which brings together a winning amount of force at a given place and time.

Positioning

SUN TZU SAID:

Learn from the history of successful battles. 1
First, you should control the situation, not try to win.
If you adjust to the enemy, you will find a way to win.
The opportunity to win does not come from yourself.
The opportunity to win comes from your enemy.

[6]You must pick good battles.
You can control them until you can win.
You cannot win them until the enemy enables your victory.

[9]We say:
You see the opportunity for victory; you don't create it.

Awaiting Opportunities

1 Sun Tzu's strategy teaches that competitive contests are always won because one competitor leaves an opening for the other. Because of this, our first responsibility should be to control the situation. We can then adjust to our opponents' positions to utilize any openings that they leave. This creates the opportunity to advance successfully.

The Chinese concept *zhan* is translated as "battle." However, it doesn't mean conflict. It means meeting opponents or challenges. It is any point of comparison where we are measured against others.

You leverage opportunities that arise from the dynamics of the competitive environment. You don't create those opportunities.

You are sometimes unable to win. 2
You must then defend.
You will eventually be able to win.
You must then attack.
Defend when you have insufficient strength.
Attack when you have a surplus of strength.

7You must defend yourself well.
Save your forces and dig in.
You must attack well.
Move your forces when you have a clear advantage.

11You must always protect yourself until you can completely
triumph.

Some may see how to win. 3
However, they cannot position their forces where they must.
This demonstrates limited ability.

4Some can struggle to a victory and the whole world may
praise their winning.
This also demonstrates a limited ability.

6Win as easily as picking up a fallen hair.
Don't use all of your forces.
See the time to move.
Don't try to find something clever.
Hear the clap of thunder.
Don't try to hear something subtle.

2 Decisions about attacking and defending are automatic. We initially and continually use our resources to defend what we have. We never attack unless we have more resources than we need to defend. Then, if we see a clear opportunity—one in which we cannot lose—then we must attack. Attacking here implies advancing, moving forward, moving into new territory, or expanding.

In the original Chinese, defense is associated with staying in place while improving a position out of basic weakness. Attack, in contrast, implies movement or action while using an opportunity from a position of strength.

Success depends totally upon our ability to protect ourselves and survive long enough for an opportunity to present itself.

3 When an opportunity presents itself, we must first recognize it. This requires vision. Then we must move a lot of resources to the right place to take advantage of the opportunity.

The failure here is in picking difficult—that is, costly—conflicts. Success under these conditions is too expensive, even if we win. We must choose positions that are easily and inexpensively obtained.

Sun Tzu taught that the world is full of opportunities. We must choose only the easiest contests most certain of success. The "time to move" is when the trends are in our favor. The "clap of thunder" means a clear, obvious sign. Sun Tzu used the metaphor of sight for vision and sound for knowledge. We must be careful not to imagine opportunities where they don't exist.

[12]Learn from the history of successful battles.
Victory goes to those who make winning easy.
A good battle is one that you will obviously win.
It doesn't take intelligence to win a reputation.
It doesn't take courage to achieve success.

[17]You must win your battles without effort.
Avoid difficult struggles.
Fight when your position must win.
You always win by preventing your defeat.

[21]You must engage only in winning battles.
Position yourself where you cannot lose.
Never waste an opportunity to defeat your enemy.

[24]You win a war by first assuring yourself of victory.
Only afterward do you look for a fight.
Outmaneuver the enemy before the first battle and then
fight to win.

When Sun Tzu refers to "history," he means the past, but he also means the statistical probability of success. When it is a question of survival, we must always bet on certainties. If we don't, we will eventually have a run of bad luck that will cost us everything. *Bing-fa* is a patient, careful philosophy that doesn't force success.

The two key ideas—winning without effort and attacking only when you will win—are intimately connected. We always win by preventing our defeat because good defense allows us to be extremely particular about picking our battles.

When the opposition eventually makes a mistake and leaves us an opening for developing our position, we must act. Life is full of opportunities, but no opportunity can ever be wasted.

It is all about winning over the long term—winning the war, not just a confrontation. You can win a difficult battle. No one wins difficult wars—everyone loses. We must keep the costs low and the potential returns high if we expect to be truly successful.

You must make good use of war. 4
Study military philosophy and the art of defense.
You can control your victory or defeat.

⁴This is the art of war:
"1.   Discuss the distances.
2.   Discuss your numbers.
3.   Discuss your calculations.
4.   Discuss your decisions.
5.   Discuss victory.

¹⁰The ground determines the distance.
The distance determines your numbers.
Your numbers determine your calculations.
Your calculations determine your decisions.
Your decisions determine your victory."

¹⁵Creating a winning war is like balancing a coin of gold
against a coin of silver.
Creating a losing war is like balancing a coin of silver
against a coin of gold.

Winning a battle is always a matter of people. 5
You pour them into battle like a flood of water pouring into
a deep gorge.
This is a matter of positioning.

♦ ♦ ♦

4 Making good use of war, in the context of positioning, means making good choices about our battleground. When we choose our ground, we decide our eventual success or failure.

The positioning test calculates the value of a possible move. Starting with distance, we decide how quickly we can move to a certain place. Small forces have the advantage of speed. Next is the amount of resources we can move. Large organizations have an advantage here. By calculating the future balance of forces at a given distant place and future time, we see which positions are winnable.

When we identify which organization can focus the most resources at a particular position at a specific time, we can know which of two competitors will win that position (*Figure 17, page 60*). The science of *classical strategy* requires that we always make this calculation before we make a decision about a making a competitive move.

A competitive situation is dynamic. Competitors are constantly moving resources into different positions. The first secret of success is concentrating our resources in the best possible positions while our opponents pick worse locations or use weaker concentrations.

5 This chapter on positioning ends with preview of the topic of the next chapter, momentum. Putting ourselves in the right place at the right time with the right resources is a start, but our success still depends on human performance, and that requires momentum.

Related Articles from *Sun Tzu's Playbook*

In this fourth chapter, Sun Tzu explains the process for advancing positions. To learn the step-by-step techniques involved, we recommend the Sun Tzu's Art of War Playbook *articles listed below.*

1.1.2 Defending Positions: how we defend our current positions until new positions are established.

1.2 Subobjective Positions: the subjective and objective aspects of a position.

1.3.1 Competitive Comparison: competition as the comparison of positions.

1.7 Competitive Power: the sources of superiority in challenges.

1.8 Progress Cycle: the adaptive loop by which positions are advanced.

1.8.1 Creation and Destruction: the creation and destruction of competitive positions.

1.8.2 The Adaptive Loop: the continual reiteration of position analysis.

3.0.0 Identifying Opportunities: the use of opportunities to advance a position.

3.2 Opportunity Creation: how change creates opportunities.

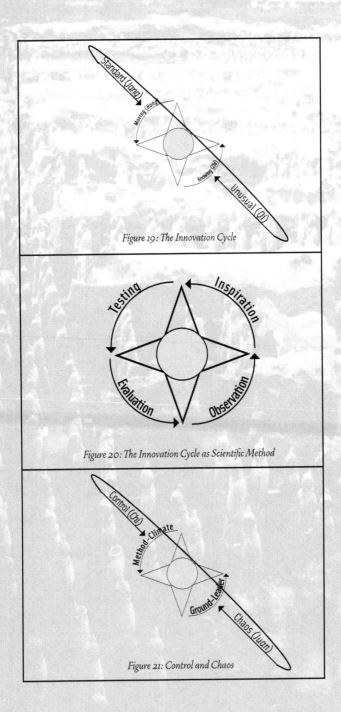

Figure 19: The Innovation Cycle

Figure 20: The Innovation Cycle as Scientific Method

Figure 21: Control and Chaos

Chapter 5

Momentum: Innovation

Sun Tzu entitled this chapter *shi*, "force," but in *bing-fa*, the character used, *shi*, is more complicated than simple power. It means putting people and events in motion in such a way that they become unstoppable. This idea is captured better by the English term "momentum." However, what interests Sun Tzu is not just momentum but the process by which it is created. This process is a systematic approach of combining standard practices with new methods to create what we call innovation (*Figure 19*). Battling with innovation simultaneously undermines an opponent's movement and knowledge.

Sun Tzu explains that standards and surprise—that is, innovation—depend on one another and that there are an infinite number of paths to innovation. He uses the metaphors of music, color, and flavor as metaphors for the three skills of knowledge (listening), foresight (aiming), and testing (moving). These are the three areas where innovation is the most important. They map to the first three steps of the scientific method (*Figure 20*). Knowledge is observation, foresight is creating a hypothesis, and movement is conducting an experiment. The pressure of innovation in this cycle must be released by timing when it is most needed.

The text then addresses the chaotic nature of all competitive movements. Though we cannot eliminate this chaos, we can control it, just as we use the chaos of innovation to disrupt the control of our opponents' plans (*Figure 21*).

Momentum

You control a large group the same as you control a few. 1
You just divide their ranks correctly.
You fight a large army the same as you fight a small one.
You only need the right position and communication.
You may meet a large enemy army.
You must be able to sustain an enemy attack without being
defeated.
You must correctly use both surprise and direct action.
Your army's position must increase your strength.
Troops flanking an enemy can smash them like eggs.
You must correctly use both strength and weakness.

It is the same in all battles. 2
You use a direct approach to engage the enemy.
You use surprise to win.

4You must use surprise for a successful invasion.
Surprise is as infinite as the weather and land.
Surprise is as inexhaustible as the flow of a river.

Innovation

1 This chapter starts by emphasizing that the rules of competition don't change with the size of an organization. What becomes more difficult in larger-sized organizations is positioning—that is, the concentration forces at an advantageous location—and communication. While *bing-fa* teaches that we should only go after positions where the balance of forces is so totally in our favor that our opponents surrender, it recognizes that more balanced confrontations or battles do occur. Specifically, we can be the target of an attack. In these situations, *xing* (positioning) is critical, but so is *qi jang*, the concept of innovation, and a third concept called *xu sat*, "weakness and strength," the topic of the next chapter.

2 What we translate as "surprise" is *qi*, literally "the unusual" or "the odd." Its opposite, *jang*, meaning "standard," is the direct approach the people expect. In *bing-fa*, *jang* makes *qi* possible.

As an attack on expectations, or knowledge, the unusual is required to move into new areas. The unlimited potential of *qi* arises from the infinite variety of ground and constantly changing trends.

7You can be stopped and yet recover the initiative.
You must use your days and months correctly.

9If you are defeated, you can recover.
You must use the four seasons correctly.

11There are only a few notes in the scale.
Yet you can always rearrange them.
You can never hear every song of victory.

14There are only a few basic colors.
Yet you can always mix them.
You can never see all the shades of victory.

17There are only a few flavors.
Yet you can always blend them.
You can never taste all the flavors of victory.

20You fight with momentum.
There are only a few types of surprises and direct actions.
Yet you can always vary the ones you use.
There is no limit to the ways you can win.

24Surprise and direct action give birth to each other.
They are like a circle without end.
You cannot exhaust all their possible combinations!

Surging water flows together rapidly. 3
Its pressure washes away boulders.
This is momentum.

The secret to regaining lost momentum is innovation, combining standards surprises. Rebuilding momentum requires time.

The power of innovation also allows us to recover from failure, but this requires continuous improvement over longer periods of time.

Though Sun Tzu's description of rearranging components to create *qi jang* innovations is poetic, it represents three steps in a process. The first step is *zhi*, knowledge, symbolized in *bing-fa* by sound.

The next step in the creative process is *jian*, that is, vision, which in Sun Tzu's system means foresight, seeing into heaven, or, in this context, inspiration, which is symbolized by sight.

The final step evaluates the movement and positioning that arise from the first two steps. This is the idea of testing, which is symbolized by flavor or smell, the idea of tasting.

Success comes from developing *shi*, momentum. *Shi*, in turn, comes from combining proven practices and novel ideas into innovation. Innovation is always possible because a few basic components can always be combined in so many different ways.

Sun Tzu teaches that novel ideas only arise from standards and new standards result only from trials of new ideas. Together, they create the infinite variety of innovation.

3 Water is *bing-fa's* metaphor for change. *Shi* (momentum) arising from *qi jang* (innovation) is a force for changing positions. Specifically, it eliminates obstacles that stand in the way of progress.

4A hawk suddenly strikes a bird.
Its contact alone kills the prey.
This is timing.

7You must fight only winning battles.
Your momentum must be overwhelming.
Your timing must be exact.

10Your momentum is like the tension of a bent crossbow.
Your timing is like the pulling of a trigger.

War is very complicated and confusing. 4
Battle is chaotic.
Nevertheless, you must not allow chaos.

4War is very sloppy and messy.
Positions turn around.
Nevertheless, you must never be defeated.

7Chaos gives birth to control.
Fear gives birth to courage.
Weakness gives birth to strength.

10You must control chaos.
This depends on your planning.
Your men must brave their fears.
This depends on their momentum.

14You have strengths and weaknesses.
These come from your position.

The concept translated as "timing" is *jie*, which literally means restraint or control. *Jie* (restraint) is the philosophical counterpart to *shi* (force), but it means holding back force until the right time.

Success requires the overwhelming force created by innovation, and it requires restraint, but "exact timing" in the Chinese is literally "brief restraint" meaning we can't wait too long.

The sense here is that the force of momentum and innovation must be held back briefly in order to be released effectively at the right time.

4 The dynamic environment of competition is inherently unpredictable. Sun Tzu calls it *juan*, chaos, in the same sense as modern chaos theory. It is unpredictable, but it can be controlled.

The terms used for "sloppy" and "messy" mean literally "muddy" and "cloudy," using water as the symbol for change. The idea is that we should expect our position, *xing*, to constantly change.

The principle that tames chaos is *chi*, control. The brave control the cowardly. The strong control the weak. In other words, it is our character that determines our reaction to chaos.

The planning that controls chaos is literally "the count" or "number," meaning the balance of forces. The balance between "cowardice" and "bravery" is determined by our *shi*, force of momentum, which is created by unleashing innovation at the right time.

Finally, the factor that determines if we are weak or strong is our position, *xing*, the place we hold in the contested field.

[16]You must force the enemy to move to your advantage.
Use your position.
The enemy must follow you.
Surrender a position.
The enemy must take it.
You can offer an advantage to move him.
You can use your men to move him.
You can use your strength to hold him.

You want a successful battle. 5
To do this, you must seek momentum.
Do not just demand a good fight from your people.
You must pick good people and then give them momentum.

[5]You must create momentum.
You create it with your men during battle.
This is comparable to rolling trees and stones.
Trees and stones roll because of their shape and weight.
Offer men safety and they will stay calm.
Endanger them and they will act.
Give them a place and they will hold.
Round them up and they will march.

[13]You make your men powerful in battle with momentum.
This should be like rolling round stones down over a high,
steep cliff.
Momentum is critical.

✦ ✦ ✦

We want our opponents to react and move based on our decisions. The entire point of using the force of momentum is to seize the initiative and take control of the situation. In doing this, we leverage our position. We change our position to continually keep our opponents off balance. Since we plan our surprises ahead of time, we can lure our opponents into traps (*gui gai*). Our movements can also be designed to manipulate our opponents, forcing them to fight against our strengths.

5 Notice that none of Sun Tzu's methods involve simply exhorting people to work harder or do better. We pick good people but then we make them successful by creating a certain state of mind. *Shi* (momentum) is primarily a psychological force.

We create momentum within our organization by understanding human nature. Once we understand human psychology, we can use our tools—expected moves (*jang*), surprise (*qi*), restraint (*jie*), and so on—to give people the required sense of momentum. Sun Tzu pares down human psychology to a basic form of self-interest that reacts predictably to certain situations. We can use conditions of safety, danger, position, and a sense of belonging to create the response in people that we desire.

This lesson echoes the last lesson in the previous chapter. Both teach that these forces—positioning and momentum—empower people. Both forces are like gravity, with positioning acting on water (change), and momentum on stones, (stability).

Related Articles from *Sun Tzu's Playbook*

In his fifth chapter, Sun Tzu explains the process for creating momentum. To learn the step-by-step techniques involved, we recommend the Sun Tzu's Art of War Playbook *articles listed below.*

7.3.2 Elemental Rearrangement: seeing invention as rearranging proven elements.

7.3.3 Creative Innovation: the more advanced methods for innovation.

7.4 Competitive Timing: the role of timing in creating momentum.

7.4.1 Timing Methods: the three simplest methods of controlling timing.

7.4.2 Momentum Timing: the relative value of momentum at various times in a campaign.

7.4.3 Interrupting Patterns: how repetition creates patterns for surprise.

7.5 Momentum Limitations: the implications of momentum's temporary nature.

7.5.1 Momentum Conversion: converting momentum into positions with more value.

7.5.2 The Spread of Innovation: the spread of innovation to advance our position.

7.6 Productive Competition: using momentum to produce more resources.

7.6.1 Resource Discovery: using innovation to create value from seemingly worthless resources.

7.6.2 Ground Creation: the creation of new competitive ground to be successful.

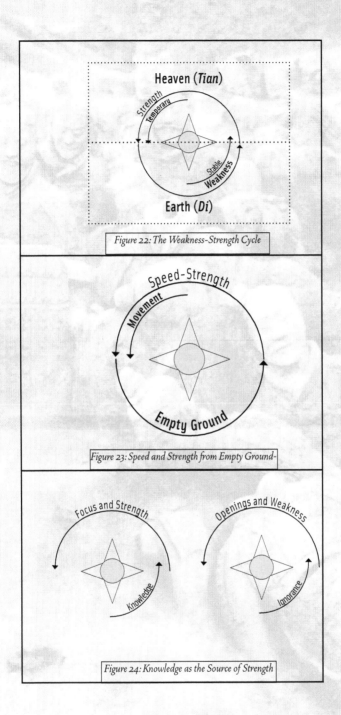

Heaven (*Tian*)

Strength
Temporary

Stable
Weakness

Earth (*Di*)

Figure 22: The Weakness-Strength Cycle

Speed-Strength

Movement

Empty Ground

Figure 23: Speed and Strength from Empty Ground-

Focus and Strength

Openings and Weakness

Knowledge

Ignorance

Figure 24: Knowledge as the Source of Strength

Chapter 6

Weakness and Strength

The two opposing and complementary concepts that are the topic of this chapter, *xu* and *sat*, are difficult to translate. *Xu* is generally translated as weakness, but it literally means false, worthless, empty, and hollow. *Sat* is translated as strength, but it literally means real, wealthy, honest, and solid. Together these concepts describe the mechanism by which we avoid conflict and turn problems into opportunities. The contrasting ideas of *xu* (weakness, emptiness) and *sat* (strength, fullness) are united. Strength equals abundance and is associated with heaven as a temporary state. Weakness equals need and is associated with the ground as a stable state (*Figure 22*).

Sun Tzu begins addressing this complex idea by explaining that an army that arrives at an empty battlefield is naturally stronger than one that moves into an area occupied by other forces. He then continues to explain that movement through empty terrain is speedier and that both attack and defense are easier when you are working against emptiness or weakness (*Figure 23*).

Sun Tzu then explains the relationship between knowledge and ignorance and strength and weakness (*figure 24*). He tells how to focus our strengths against the weaknesses in the opposition's formations by keeping our plans a secret. Then he extends the discussion to consider how secrecy creates opportunities to exploit weakness. Sun Tzu then summarizes weakness and strength by applying these concepts to planning, action, position, and battle.

Weakness and Strength

SUN TZU SAID:

Always arrive first to the empty battlefield to await the 1
enemy at your leisure.
After the battleground is occupied and you hurry to it,
fighting is more difficult.

3You want a successful battle.
Move your men, but not into opposing forces.

5You can make the enemy come to you.
Offer him an advantage.
You can make the enemy avoid coming to you.
Threaten him with danger.

9When the enemy is fresh, you can tire him.
When he is well fed, you can starve him.
When he is relaxed, you can move him.

Competitive Relativity

1 *Xu* (weakness, emptiness) and *sat* (strength, fullness) are conditions. They are neither good nor bad in themselves, but they create opportunities. The emptiness (*xu*) of the ground (*di*) is an opportunity. Fullness (*sat*) of the ground is not.

Success, in general, requires movement (*hang*) toward emptiness (*xu*), weakness, or need and away from fullness (*sat*) and strength.

In the last chapter, Sun Tzu discussed the idea of controlling our opponent's movement. Here, he continues that discussion by explaining how to use emptiness (*xu*) to attract an opponent's attack and apparent fullness (*sat*) to prevent an attack.

Fullness (*sat*) also means being rested, well fed, and relaxed. *Bing-fa* teaches us that all fullness is a temporary condition. The fullness of an opponent is a condition that we can work to change.

Leave any place without haste. **2**
Hurry to where you are unexpected.
You can easily march hundreds of miles without tiring.
To do so, travel through areas that are deserted.
You must take whatever you attack.
Attack when there is no defense.
You must have walls to defend.
Defend where it is impossible to attack.

9Be skilled in attacking.
Give the enemy no idea where to defend.

11Be skillful in your defense.
Give the enemy no idea where to attack.

Be subtle! Be subtle! **3**
Arrive without any clear formation.
Ghostly! Ghostly!
Arrive without a sound.
You must use all your skill to control the enemy's decisions.

6Advance where he can't defend.
Charge through his openings.
Withdraw where the enemy cannot chase you.
Move quickly so that he cannot catch you.

2. *Xu sat* (emptiness/fullness) conditions affect the economics of competition. Since the ground (*di*) supplies our strength and since filling the ground creates strength, we must leave established areas slowly and establish new ones quickly. Movement (*hang*) through emptiness (*xu*) is quicker and less expensive than movement through full (*xu*) areas. We attack the emptiness of *xu*, but, since our first responsibility is to defend (*shou*), we build walls to create fullness, which makes a position (*xing*) that is impossible to attack.

Our ability to take territory from our opponents depends on identifying areas that are empty, needy, and, therefore, undefended.

Our ability to hold a territory depends upon our ability to fill or satisfy that area so that there are no openings for the competition.

3 Contradicting the fashion of noisy self-promotion, Sun Tzu teaches us to keep quiet and be invisible to the enemy. Sound is *bing-fa's* metaphor for knowledge (*zhi*). Strength (*sat*) is full knowledge, so we must keep our opponents empty (*xu*) and ignorant. We control others by controlling their knowledge of our actions.

We have two choices about how we can move toward the emptiness of *xu*. We can attack, that is, move into enemy territory, but only if the enemy leaves us an opening (*xu*). We can also elude the enemy, moving into emptiness (*xu*) more quickly than he can follow.

[10]Always pick your own battles.
The enemy can hide behind high walls and deep trenches.
Do not try to win by fighting him directly.
Instead, attack a place that he must recapture.
Avoid the battles that you don't want.
You can divide the ground and yet defend it.
Don't give the enemy anything to win.
Divert him by coming to where you defend.

Make other men take a position while you take none. 4
Then focus your forces where the enemy divides his forces.
Where you focus, you unite your forces.
When the enemy divides, he creates many small groups.
You want your large group to attack one of his small ones.
Then you have many men where the enemy has but a few.
Your larger force can overwhelm his smaller one.
Then go on to the next small enemy group.
You can take them one at a time.

You must keep the place that you have chosen as a 5 battleground a secret.
The enemy must not know.
Force the enemy to prepare his defense in many places.
You want the enemy to defend many places.
Then you can choose where to fight.
His forces will be weak there.

In *bing-fa*, we always have a choice of ground (*di*). We must see our position (*xing*) as dynamic, something we can shift at will. The principle of emptiness (*xu*) and fullness (*sat*) determines where we put our resources. We never move against our opponents' strong points. Instead, we look for places that they need and that they have left needy and undefended. "Dividing a territory" means focusing on a small segment. If we don't want a confrontation, we empty an area, leaving the opposition nothing to win there.

4 The principle of *xu sat* (emptiness/fullness) also applies to our positioning (*xing*). Positioning brings forces together, uniting them into *quan* (completeness) and giving them focus (*zhuan*). The opposite of complete (*quan*) is broken (*po*). Most organizations protect too much territory, forcing them to divide (*fen*) their efforts, making their forces weak and positions empty (*xu*). The solution to this is to position our forces together and focus them in a specific, small enemy area. Positioning a whole, solid (*quan sat*) force against a divided, empty (*po xu*) force is always successful.

5 We use emptiness (*xu*) in the realm of knowledge (*zhi*) about our battleground (*di*) to cause our opponents to divide (*po*) their forces. If we keep the ground (*di*) that we have chosen for our focus (*zhuan*) a secret, our opponents must defend (*shou*) many different grounds. Without a focus (*zhuan*), organizations always spread out, defending (*shou*) too many different places. This process naturally creates many openings and weak (*xu*) points.

7If he reinforces his front lines, he depletes his rear.
If he reinforces his rear, he depletes his front.
If he reinforces his right flank, he depletes his left.
If he reinforces his left flank, he depletes his right.
Without knowing the place of attack, he cannot prepare.
Without knowing the right place, he will be weak everywhere.

13The enemy has weak points.
Prepare your men against them.
He has strong points.
Make his men prepare themselves against you.

You must know the battleground. 6
You must know the time of battle.
You can then travel a thousand miles and still win the battle.

4The enemy should not know the battleground.
He shouldn't know the time of battle.
His left flank will be unable to support his right.
His right will be unable to support his left.
His front lines will be unable to support his rear.
His rear will be unable to support his front.
His support is distant even if it is only ten miles away.
What unknown place can be close?

12You control the balance of forces.
The enemy may have many men but they are superfluous.
How can they help him to victory?

Shifting resources around within a large area is not the same process as positioning (*xing*) and does not create wholeness (*quan*) or focus (*zhuan*). The term *zhuan* literally means "to concentrate on" or "to specialize." Movement (*hang*) without focus (*zhuan*) is the opposite of positioning. Continually shifting positions without purpose is costly and does nothing to create strength.

The choices we make are ultimately simple. We focus our resources on areas of need, that is, emptiness (*xu*). We don't let competitors know where we are focusing so that they cannot counteract our focus in time to be effective against us.

6 Together, the ground (*di*) and heaven (*tian*) define the place and time of positioning (*xing*). Movement is never wasted when based on knowledge (*zhi*) of the right place and time.

Ignorance—empty or false knowledge (*xu zhi*)—changes the positioning test (*xing kao*) that we normally make (see 4:4.4) to calculate the balance of forces. In this calculation, the distance is usually critical. However, if opponents don't know the place and time (*di tian*), distance becomes irrelevant. When we choose our focus (*zhuan*), our opportunity is only temporary, but the fact that we know the focus—and our opponents do not—gives us all the advantage that we need, irrespective of distance.

Similarly, an understanding of emptiness and fullness in space and time renders size—the other significant number in the positioning test—irrelevant. We force the enemy to react to us.

[15]We say:

You must let victory happen.

[17]The enemy may have many men.

You can still control him without a fight.

When you form your strategy, know the strengths and 7
weaknesses of your plan.

When you execute a plan, know how to manage both action
and inaction.

When you take a position, know the deadly and the winning
grounds.

When you enter into battle, know when you have too many
or too few men.

[5]Use your position as your war's centerpiece.

Arrive at the battle without a formation.

Don't take a position in advance.

Then even the best spies can't report it.

Even the wisest general cannot plan to counter you.

Take a position where you can triumph using superior numbers.

Keep opposing forces ignorant.

Everyone should learn your location after your position has
given you success.

No one should know how your location gives you a winning
position.

Make a successful battle one from which the enemy cannot
recover.

You must continually adjust your position to his position.

We must be opportunistic. We must take what opponents give us and accept what we are given instead of looking for fights.

Our understanding of emptiness and fullness, wholeness and division, and place and time give us the critical local advantage.

7 The principles of *xu sat* (emptiness/fullness) affect every step in our use of the competitive cycle. Our knowledge (*zhi*) of *xu sat* exposes the strengths and weaknesses of our competitive vision (*jian*). In executing our vision, *xu sat* tells us when to move (*hang*) and when to stay where we are. When we concentrate our forces at a position (*xing*), *xu sat* allows us to pick the right place and time. Our opponent's ignorance of that place and time determines the relative balance of power.

In competition, the most critical step in the four-step cycle of knowledge, vision, movement, and positioning is the last step, positioning (*xing*). Positioning requires focusing our efforts and resources at a specific place and time. This cannot be done too soon because it gives our opponents the knowledge (*zhi*) from which to create the appropriate reaction to counter our efforts. Positioning is the end result of all our other competitive skills. To serve us, the position on which we focus must be empty (*xu*) when we get there. If our potential opponents cannot guess our plans, they cannot move to fill the openings that we see. Done correctly, this approach makes us so powerful at the chosen place and time that our concentration of forces is unassailable and certain of complete success. Opponents cannot react quickly enough to undermine our efforts because our efforts were based on their positioning.

Manage your military position like water. 8
Water takes every shape.
It avoids the high and moves to the low.
Your war can take any shape.
It must avoid the strong and strike the weak.
Water follows the shape of the land that directs its flow.
Your forces follow the enemy who determines how you win.

[8]Make war without a standard approach.
Water has no consistent shape.
If you follow the enemy's shifts and changes, you can always
find a way to win.
We call this shadowing.

[12]Fight five different campaigns without a firm rule for victory.
Use all four seasons without a consistent position.
Your timing must be sudden.
A few weeks determine your failure or success.

✦ ✦ ✦

8 Water (*shui*) is Sun Tzu's analogy for change. Water is perfect for this chapter's focus on the dynamics of competitive movement and positioning. The flow of water toward emptiness (*xu*) reflects the nature of opportunism. As positions of weakness and strength change, we must continuously shift toward the weakness and emptiness. We do not determine where that weakness is but react to it. Others' decisions are what create the emptiness we seek.

Water also symbolizes changing our competitive methods. In dynamic situations, we cannot repeat the same specific moves that we have already used. We must react to our opposition without making our moves predictable. As opponents move, we must trust that they will eventually create opportunities for us.

Water is the element of *tian*—heaven—which controls changing conditions over time. Changes in trends generate unique opportunities. We must react quickly before our window of opportunity closes. Our success or failure is determined by time.

Related Articles from *Sun Tzu's Playbook*

In chapter six, Sun Tzu explains how to find opportunities by leveraging opposites. To learn the step-by-step techniques involved, we recommend the Sun Tzu's Art of War Playbook *articles listed below.*

1.2.1 Competitive Landscapes: the arenas in which rivals jockey for position.

1.2.2 Exploiting Exploration: how competitive landscapes are searched and positions utilized.

1.2.3 Position Complexity: how strategic positions arise from interactions in complex environments.

1.3.1 Competitive Comparison: competition as the comparison of positions.

2.4 Contact Networks: the range of contacts needed to create perspective.

2.4.1 Ground Perspective: getting information on a new competitive arena.

2.4.2 Climate Perspective: getting perspective on temporary external conditions.

2.4.3 Command Perspective: developing sources for understanding decision-makers.

2.4.4 Methods Perspective: developing contacts who understand best practices.

2.4.5 Mission Perspective: how we develop and use a perspective on motivation.

2.5 The Big Picture: building big-picture strategic awareness.

2.6 Knowledge Leverage: getting competitive value out of knowledge.

2.7 Information Secrecy: the role of limiting information in controlling relationships.

3.2.3 Complementary Opposites: the dynamics of balance from opposing forces.

3.2.4 Emptiness and Fullness: rules on the transformations between emptiness and fullness.

3.2.5 Dynamic Reversal: how situations reverse themselves naturally.

3.5 Strength and Weakness: six rules regarding openings created by the strength of others.

3.6 Leveraging Subjectivity: openings between subjective and objective positions.

3.7 Defining the Ground: redefining a competitive arena to create relative mismatches.

3.8 Strategic Matrix Analysis: two-dimensional representations of strategic space.

4.7 Competitive Weakness: how certain opportunities can bring out our weaknesses.

4.7.1 Command Weaknesses: the character flaws of leaders and how to exploit them.

4.7.2 Group Weaknesses: organizational weakness and where groups fail.

6.7 Tailoring to Conditions: overcoming opposition using conditions in the environment.

6.7.1 Form Adjustments: adapting responses based on the form of the ground.

6.7.2 Size Adjustments: adapting responses based on comparing size of forces.

6.7.3 Strength Adjustments: adapting responses based on unity of opposing forces.

6.8 Competitive Psychology: improving competitive psychology even in adversity and failure.

6.8.1 Adversity and Creativity: how we use adversity to spark our creativity.

6.8.2 Strength in Adversity: using adversity to increase a group's unity and focus.

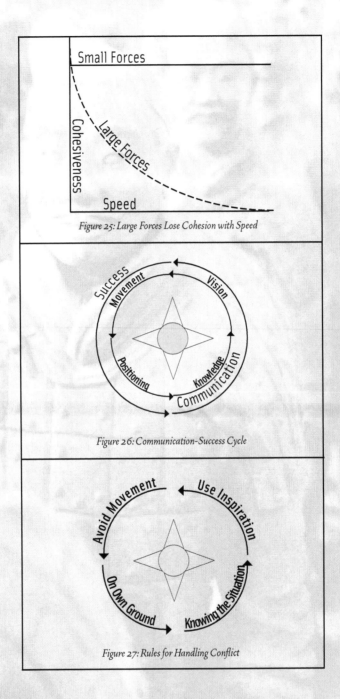

Figure 25: Large Forces Lose Cohesion with Speed

Figure 26: Communication-Success Cycle

Figure 27: Rules for Handling Conflict

Chapter 7

Armed Conflict: Direct Confrontation

In this chapter, Sun Tzu makes it clear that conflict (*zheng*) is not the most desirable path to success in competition. We can be successful in competition while avoiding confrontation and conflict. We prepare for confrontation, but our goal is always to avoid it. Sun Tzu's strategy warns against ever engaging in direct confrontation without a decisive advantage. The latter part of the chapter covers techniques for succeeding in these conflicts when they are unavoidable.

Sun Tzu begins by explaining the dangers of conflict and that it cannot be undertaken carelessly. He then explains the disasters that occur when we rush into confrontations with the enemy without proper preparation, because the cohesion of large forces breaks down when they are hurried (*Figure 25*).

When confrontations are unavoidable, he emphasizes the need for deception and the need for improved methods of communication. Good communication of knowledge and vision is the primary key to winning all battles (*Figure 26*).

Sun Tzu then addresses the proper timing for making contact with the enemy in order to control the situation. In the final section, he provides a short but critical list of rules for avoiding mistakes during contact with the enemy. All together, Sun Tzu's rules for success during conflict map well into the four-step skill cycle (*Figure 27*).

Armed Conflict

SUN TZU SAID:

Everyone uses the arts of war. 1
You accept orders from the government.
Then you assemble your army.
You organize your men and build camps.
You must avoid disasters from armed conflict.

6Seeking armed conflict can be disastrous.
Because of this, a detour can be the shortest path.
Because of this, problems can become opportunities.

9Use an indirect route as your highway.
Use the search for advantage to guide you.
When you fall behind, you must catch up.
When you get ahead, you must wait.
You must know the detour that most directly accomplishes
your plan.

14Undertake armed conflict when you have an advantage.
Seeking armed conflict for its own sake is dangerous.

Direct Confrontation

1 Sun Tzu teaches that whether we realize it or not, we all use some techniques of strategy, even if we haven't studied his system. It is natural to go through certain steps in setting goals and assembling and organizing resources. However, it is also natural—and a mistake—to seek confrontation in competitive situations.

The mistaken perception of competition (*bing*) as conflict (*zheng*) is a huge danger. To avoid conflict, we must seek our own paths or detours that open new areas to discover opportunity.

Instead of looking for conflict, we look for opportunities by moving (*hang*) along detours. As less traveled paths, detours are a form of emptiness (*xu*) and offer us the possibility of discovering opportunities that others don't know about. The only danger in moving on these paths is becoming divided, so we have to pace ourselves to keep our forces together and therefore focused.

When our advantage is certain, we can accept competitive challenges that are unavoidable, but confrontation is never a goal.

You can build up an army to fight for an advantage. 2
Then you won't catch the enemy.
You can force your army to go fight for an advantage.
Then you abandon your heavy supply wagons.

5You keep only your armor and hurry after the enemy.
You avoid stopping day or night.
You use many roads at the same time.
You go hundreds of miles to fight for an advantage.
Then the enemy catches your commanders and your army.
Your strong soldiers get there first.
Your weaker soldiers follow behind.
Using this approach, only one in ten will arrive.
You can try to go fifty miles to fight for an advantage.
Then your commanders and army will stumble.
Using this method, only half of your soldiers will make it.
You can try to go thirty miles to fight for an advantage.
Then only two out of three will get there.

18If you make your army travel without good supply lines,
your army will die.
Without supplies and food, your army will die.
If you don't save the harvest, your army will die.

2 Our efforts cannot create opportunities through conflict. In
a way, conflict is unnatural. When we have a large enough force to
win, we are too slow to catch opponents. To move quickly when we
are large, we have to abandon our resources.

The warning against fighting for advantage is similar to the warning against attacking an opponent's strong points. By definition,
when we build a larger force than that of the opposition, we are
also building a force that is slower than that of the opposition.
How does a large force catch a smaller one for a direct contest of
power? The only solution is "hurry"—that is, leaving supplies,
taking shortcuts, and pressing people to go as fast as they can. *Bing-
fa* teaches that "hurry" destroys the unity of a force, negating its
strength. Positioning, which brings forces together at a single place
and time, is the opposite of hurried pursuit. The further a force
has to hurry in pursuit, the more divided and weak it becomes. So
hurry times distance creates division, which creates weakness by
hollowing out our forces.

The worst part of "hurry" is the loss of the supply lines. This
doesn't just create weakness, it is fatal. Without providing
resources for the future, it is only a matter of time until we can no
longer compete.

²¹Do not let any of your potential enemies know what you
are planning.
Still, you must not hesitate to form alliances.
You must know the mountains and forests.
You must know where the obstructions are.
You must know where the marshes are.
If you don't, you cannot move the army.
If you don't, you must use local guides.
If you don't, you can't take advantage of the terrain.

You make war by making a false stand. 3
By finding an advantage, you can move.
By dividing and joining, you can reinvent yourself and trans-
form the situation.
You can move as quickly as the wind.
You can rise like the forest.
You can invade and plunder like fire.
You can stay as motionless as a mountain.
You can be as mysterious as the fog.
You can strike like sounding thunder.

¹⁰Divide your troops to plunder the villages.
When on open ground, dividing is an advantage.
Don't worry about organization; just move.
Be the first to find a new route that leads directly to a win-
ning plan.
This is how you are successful at armed conflict.

To contrast with hurried pursuit, Sun Tzu gives us a lesson in correct movement. Instead of looking for confrontations, we must move based on a plan. Rather than chasing our opponents, we should keep them in the dark about our intentions. Instead of seeking conflict, we should seek alliances. All movement must be based on knowledge of the ground. The most basic principle of *bing-fa* is that knowledge of the ground makes good positioning (*xing*) possible. And good positioning, not conflict, is the source of advantage or opportunity.

3 There are three techniques for making competitive progress in the face of opposition. The technique for undermining knowledge is deception —that is, misleading others about where we are going to concentrate our efforts. The technique for movement is finding an opportunity. You cannot move until you see an opportunity and have a goal. The technique for change—that is, changing the situation or the competitive balance—is redistributing and reuniting our forces. In the original Chinese, the terms used are distribute and join, but the concepts are simply more active forms of the familiar states of united or complete and divided or broken.

Unity gives us strength in confrontations and convinces others to avoid confronting us, but unity is not needed if we have no opposition. We can then spread out, dividing our time and resources among several different tasks. This allows us to get the benefit of more ground, more quickly. We can do this if we move quickly and use detours to find an advantage which makes us unassailable.

Military experience says: 4
"You can speak, but you will not be heard.
You must use gongs and drums.
You cannot really see your forces just by looking.
You must use banners and flags."

⁶You must master gongs, drums, banners, and flags.
Place people as a single unit where they can all see and hear.
You must unite them as one.
Then the brave cannot advance alone.
The fearful cannot withdraw alone.
You must force them to act as a group.

¹²In night battles, you must use numerous fires and drums.
In day battles, you must use many banners and flags.
You must position your people to control what they see and
hear.

You control your army by controlling its morale. 5
As a general, you must be able to control emotions.

³In the morning, a person's energy is high.
During the day, it fades.
By evening, a person's thoughts turn to home.
You must use your troops wisely.
Avoid the enemy's high spirits.
Strike when his men are lazy and want to go home.
This is how you master energy.

4 At this point, the topic changes from avoiding armed conflict to winning in confrontations when we can't avoid them. The first key to winning a conflict is good communication, which is defined as everyone hearing and seeing the same thing. In conflict, this is inherently difficult, so communication must be amplified.

The purpose of all strategic communication is uniting a group as one, which leads to completeness. In times of conflict and confrontation, our unity gives us strength. The language here is meant to echo the lesson earlier in the chapter about "hurry," which spreads out forces (see 7:2.10-11) rather than unifying them. Communication does the opposite, bringing forces together.

Conditions vary, but execution depends on communication, so we must be able to communicate in every situation. Part of choosing a position means considering its utility for good communication and using whatever resources are available.

5 After communication, the second most important key in confrontation is controlling emotions, spirit, or morale.

The first technique of controlling the emotional energy of *hei* is largely a matter of using the correct timing. This is an aspect of using foresight to understand trends. Strategic analysis teaches that people's emotional resilience is stronger earlier in the day and gradually grows weaker as night approaches. By extension, we can also say that people are more resolved earlier in a campaign, but that their resolve wavers over time.

¹⁰Use discipline to await the chaos of battle.
Keep relaxed to await a crisis.
This is how you master emotion.

¹³Stay close to home to await the distant enemy.
Stay comfortable to await the weary enemy.
Stay well fed to await the hungry enemy.
This is how you master power.

Don't entice the enemy when his ranks are orderly.
You must not attack when his formations are solid.
This is how you master adaptation.

⁴You must follow these military rules.
Do not take a position facing the high ground.
Do not oppose those with their backs to the wall.
Do not follow those who pretend to flee.
Do not attack the enemy's strongest men.
Do not swallow the enemy's bait.
Do not block an army that is heading home.
Leave an escape outlet for a surrounded army.
Do not press a desperate foe.
This is how you use military skills.

⧫ ⧫ ⧫

The next technique for winning in conflict is control, meaning self-discipline and self-control. In *bing-fa*, self-control means using patience and waiting while controlling our emotions.

Finally, we win in conflict by keeping ourselves whole and full. The description here echoes the temporary conditions of *sat* from 6:1.9-11. Sun Tzu calls this "mastering power." Power here is the Chinese concept of *lei*, which means "force" or "merit."

6 Finally, we look forward to the next chapter's topic, change and adaptability. Changing a situation (*see Chapter 7:3.3*) also requires avoiding opponents with control and solidity.

Adaptability is also our ability to change based upon our situation. The concept of adaptability requires us to avoid confrontations when our opponents are in a strong or controlling position. We never confront opponents when they are in a strong position. We never let enemy actions dictate the flow of events. We never force confrontations that are so costly that our opponents cannot afford to surrender. In other words, when we cannot avoid direct confrontations, we must manage them so that we have a decent chance of success. It is never just our strength that matters; it is our relationship to our opponent's weakness and strength (*xu sat*).

Related Articles from *Sun Tzu's Playbook*

In chapter seven, Sun Tzu teaches us to focus on building positions instead of on tearing down opponents. To learn the step-by-step techniques involved, we recommend the Sun Tzu's Art of War Playbook articles listed below.

1.2.1 Competitive Landscapes: the arenas in which rivals jockey for position.

1.3.1 Competitive Comparison: competition as the comparison of positions.

1.5 Competing Agents: characteristics of competitors.

1.7 Competitive Power: the sources of superiority in challenges.

1.8.1 Creation and Destruction: the creation and destruction of competitive positions.

1.9 Competition and Production: the two opposing skill sets of competition and production.

2.1.3 Strategic Deception: misinformation and disinformation in competition.

2.6 Knowledge Leverage: getting competitive value out of knowledge.

2.7 Information Secrecy: the role of secrecy in relationships.

3.1 Strategic Economics: balancing the cost and benefits of positioning.

3.1.1 Resource Limitations: the inherent limitation of strategic resources.

3.1.3 Conflict Cost: the costly nature of resolving competitive comparisons by conflict.

3.1.6 Time Limitations: understanding the time limits on opportunities.

3.7 Defining the Ground: redefining a competitive arena to create relative mismatches.

4.7 Competitive Weakness: how certain opportunities can bring out our weaknesses.

6.1.2 Prioritizing Conditions: parsing complex competitive conditions into simple responses.

6.8 Competitive Psychology: improving competitive psychology even in adversity and failure.

7.4 Competitive Timing: the role of timing in creating momentum.

7.6 Productive Competition: using momentum to produce more resources.

7.6.2 Ground Creation: the creation of new competitive ground to be successful.

8.5 Leveraging Emotions: how we use emotion to obtain rewards.

9.5.2 Avoiding Emotion: the danger of exploiting environmental vulnerabilities for purely emotion reasons.

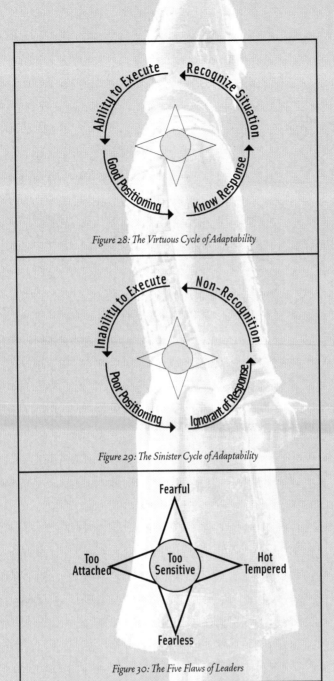

Figure 28: The Virtuous Cycle of Adaptability

Figure 29: The Sinister Cycle of Adaptability

Figure 30: The Five Flaws of Leaders

Chapter 8

Adaptability: Opportunism

The Chinese name for this chapter means literally "many changes." The concept of change or *bian* in *bing-fa* includes both our efforts to change a situation and our reaction to changing conditions. The specific topic of this chapter is the latter meaning: adjusting to changing conditions. In Sun Tzu's view, successful strategies must be dynamic. This chapter is best understood in its context as an introduction to the next three chapters, which give a great deal of information about specific situations and how to respond to them.

In the chapter's first section, Sun Tzu lists situations (covered in greater detail in several other chapters) that show the need to constantly change our plans (*Figure 28*). The next short section makes the point that we can be creative and constantly adapt our methods without being inconsistent in our results.

We can also use the dynamics of competitive situations to control our opponents' behavior. We want to encourage our opponents to make incorrect assessments and movements in response to our challenges (*Figure 29*). Sun Tzu then covers the need to address the unpredictability of opponents in planning the defense of our position.

Finally, Sun Tzu lists the five weaknesses of leaders and explains how easily these weaknesses can be exploited in the dynamics of competition. The five weaknesses map to the five key elements of *bing-fa* introduced in the first chapter (*Figure 30*).

Adaptability

Everyone uses the arts of war. 1
As a general, you get your orders from the government.
You gather your troops.
On dangerous ground, you must not camp.
Where the roads intersect, you must join your allies.
When an area is cut off, you must not delay in it.
When you are surrounded, you must scheme.
In a life-or-death situation, you must fight.
There are roads that you must not take.
There are armies that you must not fight.
There are strongholds that you must not attack.
There are positions that you must not defend.
There are government commands that must not be obeyed.

[14]Military leaders must be experts in knowing how to adapt
to find an advantage.
This will teach you the use of war.

[16]Some commanders are not good at making adjustments to
find an advantage.
They can know the shape of the terrain.
Still, they cannot find an advantageous position.

Opportunism

1 The beginning of this chapter echoes the beginning of the previous chapter in which Sun Tzu explains that it is natural to go through certain steps in setting goals, assembling resources, and so on. However, Sun Tzu teaches us that this preplanning is inherently limited because we must constantly adjust our plans to changing conditions. The situation dynamics, not our plans, often dictate what we can and cannot do. The list of situations and reactions given here is a sampling of the many such situations detailed in the next three chapters. In this context, the examples are used to illustrate the general principle that we are not free to do whatever we want in a competitive situation. Opportunism requires recognizing common competitive situations and knowing instantly how we must respond in order to be successful.

The Chinese term *tong* means "expert," "open," and "to move unobstructed," and infers being open to new ways. Expert leaders can use changes to find an advantage.

When leaders lack *tong*, the skill of openness and the ability to move freely, they can see their situation—the lay of the land—but they are handicapped by their limitations. They are not open to the possibility of finding an advantageous position.

[19]Some military commanders do not know how to adjust their methods.
They can find an advantageous position.
Still, they cannot use their men effectively.

You must be creative in your planning. 2
You must adapt to your opportunities and weaknesses.
You can use a variety of approaches and still have a consistent result.
You must adjust to a variety of problems and consistently solve them.

You can deter your potential enemy by using his 3 weaknesses against him.
You can keep your potential enemy's army busy by giving it work to do.
You can rush your potential enemy by offering him an advantageous position.

You must make use of war. 4
Do not trust that the enemy isn't coming.
Trust your readiness to meet him.
Do not trust that the enemy won't attack.
Rely only on your ability to pick a place that the enemy can't attack.

When leaders lack *zhi*, the specific knowledge of the adjustments that they must make in a specific situation, seeing the situation is not enough. Without the knowledge of how to respond, they cannot use their resources properly.

2 Here, Sun Tzu is telling us that despite the need for a specific type of response, creativity is still a vital part of our approach. We can vary our specific methods despite the need for a clear-cut type of action. Our goal must be consistent results, but we must adjust our responses to the situation to achieve that goal. In competitive situations, consistent actions never yield consistent results.

3 We must always take the initiative in every situation. Rather than responding to our opponents' moves, we must force them to react to our moves. To do this, we must understand their needs or weaknesses. Our opponents are motivated by the emotions of fear and greed. In the upcoming chapter, we will be given many specific examples of how to understand the competition's motives.

4 Skill in adaptability means that we are always prepared for the worst. Strategy demands that we assume that our competition is every bit as capable as we are. As the situation changes, we must assume that the competition knows how to take advantage of it. The secret to long-term success is survival. This means that we must always be looking for ways in which opponents may attack us.

You can exploit five different faults in a leader. 5
If he is willing to die, you can kill him.
If he wants to survive, you can capture him.
He may have a quick temper.
You can then provoke him with insults.
If he has a delicate sense of honor, you can disgrace him.
If he loves his people, you can create problems for him.
In every situation, look for these five weaknesses.
They are common faults in commanders.
They always lead to military disaster.

[11]To overturn an army, you must kill its general.
To do this, you must use these five weaknesses.
You must always look for them.

In the first chapter, Sun Tzu listed the five qualities of a leader. He said that leaders must be smart, trustworthy, caring, brave, and strict. Here, these five characteristics in their extremes become flaws. Bravery becomes fearlessness, allowing a leader to become too aggressive. Intelligence becomes fearfulness which allows capture. Strictness becomes bad temper, which can be provoked. Trustworthiness becomes a "delicate sense of honor," which can be embarrassed. Caring for people becomes love of individuals, which hurts the organization. As leaders, we must avoid all extremes. As competitors, we must look for these weaknesses.

The chapter ends with this lesson on leadership because adaptability is primarily a decision-making skill. Our strengths and flaws as individuals directly affect the adjustments we can make.

♦ ♦ ♦

Related Articles from *Sun Tzu's Playbook*

In chapter eight, Sun Tzu teaches us the need to constantly adapt to the situation. To learn the step-by-step techniques involved, we recommend the Sun Tzu's Art of War Playbook articles listed below.

1.8 Progress Cycle: the adaptive loop by which positions are advanced.

1.8.1 Creation and Destruction: the creation and destruction of competitive positions.

1.8.2 The Adaptive Loop: the continual reiteration of position analysis.

1.8.3 Cycle Time: the importance of speed in feedback and reaction.

1.8.4 Probabilistic Process: the role of chance in strategic processes and systems.

4.7.1 Command Weaknesses: the character flaws of leaders and how to exploit them.

5.2.1 Choosing Adaptability: choosing actions that allow us a maximum of future flexibility.

5.2.2 Campaign Methods: the use of campaigns and their methods.

5.2.3 Unplanned Steps: distinguishing campaign adjustments from steps in a plan.

5.3 Reaction Time: the use of speed in choosing actions.

5.3.1 Speed and Quickness: the use of pace within a dynamic environment.

6.0 Situation Response: selecting the actions most appropriate to a situation.

6.1 Situation Recognition: situation recognition in making advances.

6.1.1 Conditioned Reflexes: how we develop automatic, instantaneous responses.

6.1.2 Prioritizing Conditions: parsing complex competitive conditions into simple responses.

6.2 Campaign Evaluation: how we justify continued investment in an ongoing campaign.

6.2.1 Campaign Flow: seeing campaigns as a series of situations that flow logically from one to another.

6.2.2 Campaign Goals: assessing the value of a campaign by a larger mission.

6.3 Campaign Patterns: how knowing campaign stages gives us insight into our situation.

6.5 Nine Responses: the best responses to the nine common competitive situations.

6.7 Tailoring to Conditions: overcoming opposition using conditions in the environment.

6.7.1 Form Adjustments: adapting our responses based on the form of the ground.

6.7.2 Size Adjustments: adapting responses based on the relative size of opposing forces.

6.7.3 Strength Adjustments: how to adapt responses based on the relative strength of opposing missions.

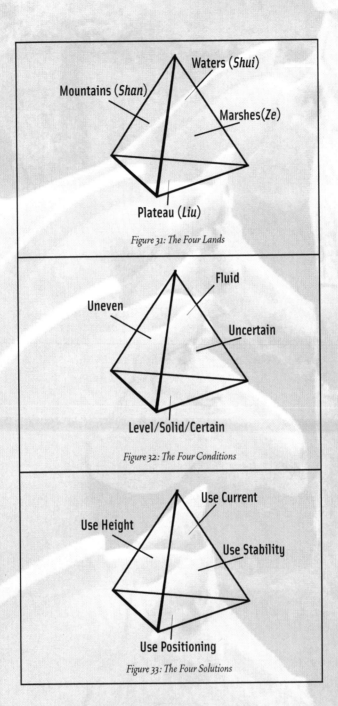

Waters (*Shui*)

Mountains (*Shan*)

Marshes(*Ze*)

Plateau (*Liu*)

Figure 31: The Four Lands

Fluid

Uneven

Uncertain

Level/Solid/Certain

Figure 32: The Four Conditions

Use Current

Use Height

Use Stability

Use Positioning

Figure 33: The Four Solutions

Chapter 9

Armed March: Exploration Strategies

This long chapter discusses four different types of competitive environments and how we utilize them in a competitive campaign. These four environments are metaphors for the general types of competitive conditions we meet in a competitive advance. Three of these environments—mountains, waters, and marshes—are defective in a way that can undermine basic positioning. The fourth environment, plateaus, is the metaphorical opposite of the other three, an ideal environment for positioning.

We can envision these possibilities as a three-sided pyramid. Each face of the pyramid represents one of the three defective grounds. The stable base of the pyramid represents the ideal competitive ground, plateaus (*Figure 31*).

Metaphorically, mountains represent uneven environments. Waters represent changing environments. Marshes represent uncertain environments. Plateaus represent level, solid, and certain environments (*Figure 32*). Each of these defective environments has a special condition that we can use to our advantage—height for mountains, current for waters, and the few stable areas for marshes. While on plateaus, correct positioning alone is paramount (*Figure 33*).

The first section of the chapter describes the four environments. Each of the four following sections focuses on one of these environments. The last section makes it clear that we must stop our advance in any environment when we run low on resources.

Armed March

SUN TZU SAID:

Anyone moving an army must adjust to the enemy. 1
When caught in the mountains, rely on their valleys.
Position yourself on the heights facing the sun.
To win your battles, never attack uphill.
This is how you position your army in the mountains.

6When water blocks you, keep far away from it.
Let the invader cross the river and wait for him.
Do not meet him in midstream.
Wait for him to get half his forces across and then take
advantage of the situation.

10You need to be able to fight.
You can't do that if you are caught in water when you meet
an invader.
Position yourself upstream, facing the sun.
Never face against the current.
Always position your army upstream when near the water.

Exploration Strategies

1 Movement depends on using the ground against opponents. Mountains are uneven areas with large variations in *xu* (emptiness) and *sat* (fullness)—powerful and weak organizations, large and small groups, important and unimportant people, etc. We move among the less powerful, but never attack into power.

Water is *bing-fa's* metaphor for change (*bian*). Think of rivers and streams as fluid areas where we have to cope with the pressures of change. Media, fashion, music, film, and high-tech industries are high-change "water" areas. Organizations competing in these areas must constantly adjust to change in order to survive.

All people find it difficult to cope with periods of change or high-change areas, but we can still compete in these situations. If we are in a high-change situation or our organization is in transition, we must use the currents, that is, pressure of trends, in our favor. We never fight against these currents. This is very much like the way we use gravity and height in the uneven areas.

15You may have to move across marshes.
Move through them quickly without stopping.
You may meet the enemy in the middle of a marsh.
You must keep on the water grasses.
Keep your back to a clump of trees.
This is how you position your army in a marsh.

21On a level plateau, take a position that you can change.
Keep the higher ground on your right and to the rear.
Keep danger in front of you and safety behind.
This is how you position yourself on a level plateau.

25You can find an advantage in all four of these situations.
Learn from the great emperor who used positioning to
conquer his four rivals.

Armies are stronger on high ground and weaker on low. 2
They are better camping on sunny southern hillsides than
on shady northern ones.
Provide for your army's health and place men correctly.
Your army will be free from disease.
Done correctly, this means victory.

6You must sometimes defend on a hill or riverbank.
You must keep on the south side in the sun.
Keep the uphill slope at your right rear.

9This will give the advantage to your army.
It will always give you a position of strength.

Marshes are a good metaphor for unstable areas and risky periods of time. Think of a financially troubled industry or uncertain market conditions as marshes. Uncertain ventures that depend on climate (*tian*)—such as farming or venture capital—are also marshes. They are not ideal competitive arenas, but we can compete in them if we find islands of stability that we can count on and protect our backs.

Think of plateaus as broad, level, stable competitive environments. Unlike the other three types of ground, these areas are the least affected by climate. In these areas, we must face our problems. Problems are where our opportunities lie. We focus on opponents.

In every situation, we must remember that no matter how difficult the environment, our opponents are on the same footing that we are. If we use better techniques, we can be more successful.

2 The mountain discussion translates "height" into a metaphor for competitive environments with lesser and more powerful positions. Big organizations and important or well-known individuals all have height. People are healthier and happier when they have the support of height, that is, the support of powerful people or large organizations.

We must defend any advantage that we have, even when we are forced to do so. We can do this by using visibility and height. In general, the idea is to always keep natural forces on our side.

According to Sun Tzu, we must use the power of fame, prestige, wealth, and any other aspect of height whenever possible.

Stop the march when the rain swells the river into rapids. 3
You may want to ford the river.
Wait until it subsides.

4All regions can have seasonal mountain streams that can
cut you off.
There are seasonal lakes.
There are seasonal blockages.
There are seasonal jungles.
There are seasonal floods.
There are seasonal fissures.
Get away from all these quickly.
Do not get close to them.
Keep them at a distance.
Maneuver the enemy close to them.
Position yourself facing these dangers.
Push the enemy back into them.

16Danger can hide on your army's flank.
There are reservoirs and lakes.
There are reeds and thickets.
There are mountain woods.
Their dense vegetation provides a hiding place.
You must cautiously search through them.
They can always hide an ambush.

3 The water discussion focuses on change and climate. Challenging periods of change can affect our progress at any time. When climate affects us, we must hold our position.

Climate changes the competitive landscape. We must be sensitive to the ways in which our particular competitive arena is affected by the current trends. Strategically, each position that we take must be a stepping-stone to a new, better position. To use stepping-stones successfully, we must avoid any dead-end positions. To identify dead-end positions, we must take into account how the competitive landscape will change over time. Many of these changes are predictable, that is, cyclical: periods of prosperity give way to periods of drought. Strategy teaches us to avoid any position that may get cut off by changes in the climate. With regard to exploring new areas for expansion, *bing-fa* is a very cautious philosophy. Strategy requires avoiding unnecessary risks. We should leave the exploration of risky opportunities for our competition.

Sun Tzu teaches us to be deeply suspicious about the new areas into which we venture. The danger in moving into new areas is that we don't know them well. This lack of knowledge is more of a problem if competitive positions in the new area are hard to see. We cannot compete unless we know where the opposition is. We must hide our own positions and movements, so we must suspect that opponents are hiding their positions and movements from us.

Sometimes, the enemy is close by but remains calm. 4
Expect to find him in a natural stronghold.
Other times he remains at a distance but provokes battle.
He wants you to attack him.

⁵He sometimes shifts the position of his camp.
He is looking for an advantageous position.

⁷The trees in the forest move.
Expect that the enemy is coming.
The tall grasses obstruct your view.
Be suspicious.

¹¹The birds take flight.
Expect that the enemy is hiding.
Animals startle.
Expect an ambush.

¹⁵Notice the dust.
It sometimes rises high in a straight line.
Vehicles are coming.
The dust appears low in a wide band.
Foot soldiers are coming.
The dust seems scattered in different areas.
The enemy is collecting firewood.
Any dust is light and settling down.
The enemy is setting up camp.

4 The marsh discussion focuses on uncertainty in the environment and how we can look for signs to uncover hidden dangers. The first sign that indicates that there is a hidden danger is found in the behavior of our opponents, who try to lure us into problems.

When opponents change their approach, it means that they've seen a hidden opportunity or discovered a secret weakness.

We often cannot see our opposition's moves directly, but we can infer them from what we see in the larger environment and what we learn from others in the environment. If we can't get good information from these sources, we must be suspicious.

We can know when the opposition is planning to surprise us by curious changes in the behavior of others. If someone knows the secret plans of our opponents, he or she will act nervously and overreact for no apparent reason.

"Dust" (*chen*) is a Chinese character showing deer kicking up dirt. As such, it represents the fundamental idea that nothing can move in the environment without leaving signs. Everything we do kicks up dirt, leaving signals that others can interpret. We can know an opponent's movement by carefully evaluating the smallest hints. Without knowing specifics, we can get an idea of opponents' actions by the amount of evidence of activity we find, the pattern of evidence, and by its increase or decrease. We have to continually monitor even the smallest rumors about competitive activity to put together a meaningful picture of activity.

Your enemy speaks humbly while building up forces. 5
He is planning to advance.

3The enemy talks aggressively and pushes as if to advance.
He is planning to retreat.

5Small vehicles exit his camp first.
They move the army's flanks.
They are forming a battle line.

8Your enemy tries to sue for peace but without offering a
treaty.
He is plotting.

10Your enemy's men run to leave and yet form ranks.
You should expect action.

12Half his army advances and the other half retreats.
He is luring you.

14Your enemy plans to fight but his men just stand there.
They are starving.

16Those who draw water drink it first.
They are thirsty.

18Your enemy sees an advantage but does not advance.
His men are tired.

5 The plateau discussion focuses on seeing through opponents'
deceptions to determine their condition and intentions.

For this reason, we shouldn't fear aggressive behavior; it is often a
smoke screen for weakness. Worry instead about feigned weakness.

Since we generally want to avoid direct confrontations, we should
be sensitive to any indication that our opponents are planning to
put up a fight. We never want to fight on an opponent's terms.

However, this doesn't mean that we should trust opponents who
want to call a truce, especially without being specific why. We want
to avoid confrontations, but we must distrust false offers.

We must also expect that opponents will try to mislead us with
actions as well as words, feigning one move while planning another.

We must suspect what looks like obvious confusion on the part of
our opponents. This is a subtler form of feint.

We can more honestly judge our opponents' condition by their associates' behavior. People often misjudge their associates' abilities.

People act based on their individual self-interest. If an opponent
has allies, we can expect those allies to act in their own self-interest.

If an opponent fails to seize an obvious opportunity, it is only
because he truly lacks the resources to do so.

²⁰Birds gather.
Your enemy has abandoned his camp.

²²Your enemy's soldiers call in the night.
They are afraid.

²⁴Your enemy's army is raucous.
The men do not take their commander seriously.

²⁶Your enemy's banners and flags shift.
Order is breaking down.

²⁸Your enemy's officers are irritable.
They are exhausted.

³⁰Your enemy's men kill their horses for meat.
They are out of provisions.

³²They don't put their pots away or return to their tents.
They are desperate.

³⁴Enemy troops appear sincere and agreeable.
But their men are slow to speak to each other.
They are no longer united.

³⁷Your enemy offers too many incentives to his men.
He is in trouble.

³⁹Your enemy gives out too many punishments.
His men are weary.

When an opponent abandons an established position, it creates activity in the environment as others move into that position.

Again, people act out of individual self-interest. If an opponent's employees are contacting us, they are worried about their jobs.

When we hear a competitor's people complaining about their management, we know their leadership is not respected.

Reorganizations are another sign of internal friction, fractures, and breakdown of unity and focus.

We shouldn't interpret middle-management hostility as aimed at us, but we should view it as frustration with their own organization.

When we see competitors selling off their assets for cash, we must assume that they are running low on resources.

When our competitors are really in bad shape, however, they can become more dangerous.

Communication is the key to coordinating alliances between organizations. People can say that they have an alliance, but if they fail to share information, no true alliance exists.

We motivate individuals to join us out of self-interest, but if we have to bribe them, they don't see the real benefit of the alliance.

Bing-fa teaches that we must make responsibilities clear, especially for new people. Overusing discipline, however, is just laziness.

[41]Your enemy first acts violently and then is afraid of your larger force.
His best troops have not arrived.

[43]Your enemy comes in a conciliatory manner.
He needs to rest and recuperate.

[45]Your enemy is angry and appears to welcome battle.
This goes on for a long time, but he doesn't attack.
He also doesn't leave the field.
You must watch him carefully.

If you are too weak to fight, you must find more men. 6
In this situation, you must not act aggressively.
You must unite your forces.
Prepare for the enemy.
Recruit men and stay where you are.

[6]You must be cautious about making plans and adjust to the enemy.
You must gather more men.

Speed is a critical factor in competition. This means that our opponents may sometimes attack before they are truly ready, as a stalling tactic, to throw us off balance and delay our progress.

If opponents can use a confrontation as a delaying tactic, they can also pretend to make peace as a delaying tactic as well.

Sometimes opponents' behavior is just confusing. Do they want a direct confrontation or not? In these cases, Sun Tzu advises that we avoid initiating any action. We must wait and see what the competition does.

6 All expansions and movements into new areas have their natural limits. When we expand into new areas, we have to know when to stop. At some point, our resources are stretched too thin to continue expanding. We must then stop and develop a defensive posture. This especially means developing more people.

No matter how successful we have been, when our people are overloaded, we have to be careful. The constraint in growth is the human span of control. People's time is our critical resource.

With new, undedicated soldiers, you can depend on them 7
if you discipline them.
They will tend to disobey your orders.
If they do not obey your orders, they will be useless.

⁴You can depend on seasoned, dedicated soldiers.
But you must avoid disciplining them without reason.
Otherwise, you cannot use them.

⁷You must control your soldiers with esprit de corps.
You must bring them together by winning victories.
You must get them to believe in you.

¹⁰Make it easy for people to know what to do by training
your people.
Your people will then obey you.
If you do not make it easy for people to know what to do,
you won't train your people.
Then they will not obey.

¹⁴Make your commands easy to follow.
You must understand the way a crowd thinks.

7 When we bring new people into an organization, we must be very clear about their responsibilities and strict in enforcing rules. By demanding a lot from our new people, we make it clear up front that we are going to challenge them to live up to our standards.

We must take a very different approach in managing our seasoned associates. As tough as we are on new people, we must give our seasoned people a great deal of freedom and trust.

People need to identify themselves with a winner. People truly become an integral part of an organization when they play a role in its success. Success in the past builds trust for the future.

Training people means giving them knowledge. This starts with understanding the organization's underlying purpose or mission, the source of the organization's unity and focus. However, it also means clearly training them in their specific roles and procedures. The more clearly we delineate their responsibilities, the better these people will work in the organization.

Strategy teaches us that simplicity of purpose and role is the key to creating a winning organizational psychology.

Related Articles from *Sun Tzu's Playbook*

In chapter nine, Sun Tzu discusses the basics of recognizing conditions in new territory. To learn the step-by-step techniques involved, we recommend the Sun Tzu's Art of War Playbook *articles listed below.*

1.1.0 Position Paths: the continuity of strategic positions over time.

1.2.2 Exploiting Exploration: how competitive landscapes are searched and positions utilized.

2.1 Information Value: knowledge and communication as the basis of strategy.

2.1.1 Information Limits: making good decisions with limited information.

2.2.1 Personal Relationships: why information depends on personal relationships.

2.2.2 Mental Models: how mental models simplify decision-making.

2.2.3 Standard Terminology: how mental models must be shared to enable communication.

2.3 Personal Interactions: making progress through personal interactions.

2.3.1 Action and Reaction: how we advance based on how others react to our actions.

2.3.2 Reaction Unpredictability: why we can never exactly predict the reactions of others.

2.3.3 Likely Reactions: the range of potential reactions in gathering information.

2.3.4 Using Questions: using questions in gathering information and predicting reactions.

4.0 Leveraging Probability: making better decisions regarding our choice of opportunities.

4.3 Leveraging Form: how we can leverage the form of our territory.

4.3.1 Tilted Forms: opportunities that are dominated by uneven forces.

4.3.2 Fluid Forms: opportunities that are dominated by fast-changing directional forces.

4.3.3 Soft Forms: opportunities that are dominated by forces that create uncertainty.

4.3.4 Neutral Forms: opportunities where the terrain has no dominant forces.

4.4 Strategic Distance: relative proximity in strategic space.

4.4.1 Physical Distance: the issues of proximity in physical space.

4.4.2 Intellectual Distance: the challenges of moving through intellectual space.

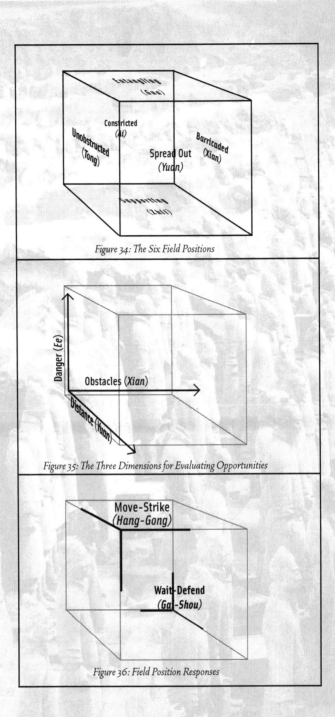

Figure 34: The Six Field Positions

Figure 35: The Three Dimensions for Evaluating Opportunities

Figure 36: Field Position Responses

Chapter 10

地 形

Field Position: Evaluating Opportunities

This chapter examines six characteristics which we use to evaluate our competitive options. "Positioning" includes all aspects of organizing our resources at a specific place and time for a competitive contest. The concept of field position involves the idea that the shape of the ground—the nature of the opportunity—determines the future potential of our forces. A given field position—literally "ground form" (*di xing*)—is evaluated based on its potential for helping us move forward or defend ourselves. Each field position acts as a stepping-stone to a future position, but, to use a field position correctly, we must understand how its characteristics affect us.

One way to visualize the six characteristics of field positions is to think about the six sides of a cube (*Figure 34*). The cube represents three dimensions (*Figure 35*). Opposing sides on the cube are opposite extremes of one dimension. We use these three dimensions—called obstacles, dangers, and distance—to evaluate the potential of a certain field position. Every position or opportunity combines these six characteristics to one degree or another, falling somewhere within the cube.

In this three-dimensional matrix, *bing-fa* defines the best positions for waiting and defending as those that are close together and less dangerous but with more obstacles. The best areas for moving or attacking are where there is more distance, more danger, and fewer obstacles (*Figure 36*).

Field Position

Some field positions are unobstructed. 1
Some field positions are entangling.
Some field positions are supporting.
Some field positions are constricted.
Some field positions give you a barricade.
Some field positions are spread out.

7You can attack from some positions easily.
Other forces can meet you easily as well.
We call these unobstructed positions.
These positions are open.
In them, be the first to occupy a high, sunny area.
Put yourself where you can defend your supply routes.
Then you will have an advantage.

Evaluating Opportunities

1 Sun Tzu lists six concepts that make up the six extremes of field position. "Unobstructed" is *tong*, the idea of openness. "Entangling" is *gua*, literally meaning "to hang." Its opposite is "supporting," *zhii*, meaning "to prop up." "Constricted," *ai*, means "narrow." "Barricaded," *xian*, means "obstructed," the opposite of *tong*, open. "Spread out" is *yuan*, meaning "far," opposite of *ai*, constricted.

The first dimension is what Sun Tzu calls "obstacles," *xian*. This dimension ranges from the barricaded position, *xian*, to the unobstructed position, *tong*. An unobstructed position or opportunity allows us to move on easily to a new opportunity, but it is open to attack. Unobstructed positions offer an advantage for movement but not defense. They are good but temporary stepping stones to better positions.

¹⁴You can attack from some positions easily.

Disaster arises when you try to return to them.

These are entangling positions.

These field positions are one-sided.

Wait until your enemy is unprepared.

You can then attack from these positions and win.

Avoid a well-prepared enemy.

You will try to attack and lose.

Since you can't return, you will meet disaster.

These field positions offer no advantage.

²⁴You cannot leave some positions without losing an advantage.

If the enemy leaves this ground, he also loses an advantage.

We call these supporting field positions.

These positions strengthen you.

The enemy may try to entice you away.

Still, hold your position.

You must entice the enemy to leave.

You then strike him as he is leaving.

These field positions offer an advantage.

³³Some field positions are constricted.

Get to these positions first.

You must fill these areas and await the enemy.

Sometimes, the enemy will reach them first.

If he fills them, do not follow him.

However, if he fails to fill them, you can go after him.

The next dimension is a stickiness that Sun Tzu calls *ee*, which is translated as "danger," but which also means "adversity" or "opposition." Its first extreme is *gua*, the entangling position. We can attack from an entangling position or opportunity, but we cannot return to it. It is dangerous because it doesn't leave us a fall-back position if our attack is unsuccessful. In business, entangling positions are common. For example, if Tupperware—built on selling at parties through a distribution network—starts selling retail, the company will find it impossible to return to its distribution network if it fails in the retail market.

The other extreme of *ee*, danger, is the supporting position. We cannot move from a supporting position and must return to it. We get stuck in entangling positions because we can't return, but we get stuck in supporting positions because the opportunities that they offer are so good that we cannot abandon them. A good example of a supporting position is that of Coca-Cola. When the company tried to introduce New Coke, it was forced to return to Classic Coke. Supporting positions are opportunities, but since field positions are meant to be stepping-stones, supporting positions represent a danger to future movement.

The next dimension, *yuan*, is that of distance. Distance gauges how broadly or narrowly we are spread out. A constricted (*ai*) position is one extreme. Strategically, a constricted opportunity is good for defense when we need to wait for a situation to develop. Constricted positions represent a concentration of resources, which cannot be easily attacked.

39Some field positions give you a barricade.
Get to these positions first.
You must occupy their southern, sunny heights in order to
await the enemy.
Sometimes the enemy occupies these areas first.
If so, entice him away.
Never go after him.

45Some field positions are too spread out.
Your force may seem equal to the enemy.
Still you will lose if you provoke a battle.
If you fight, you will not have any advantage.

49These are the six types of field positions.
Each battleground has its own rules.
As a commander, you must know where to go.
You must examine each position closely.

Some armies can be outmaneuvered. 2
Some armies are too lax.
Some armies fall down.
Some armies fall apart.
Some armies are disorganized.
Some armies must retreat.

7Know all six of these weaknesses.
They create weak timing and disastrous positions.
They all arise from the army's commander.

A barricaded (*xian*) position is the most blocked extreme of the obstacle (*xian*) dimension. The opposite of an unobstructed position, a barricaded position is good for defense but poor for movement. Like a constricted position, it requires us to wait for our opponents to attack us. Unobstructed and barricaded positions offer opposite types of opportunities, but both can be used to our advantage at the right time.

The spread-out (*yuan*) position is the furthest extreme of the distance (*yuan*) dimension and the opposite of a constricted position. A spread-out position is the poorest concentration of forces and very bad for battle but good for plundering.

Field positions are ideally stepping-stones to better positions. We have a choice about what positions we move to. Choosing the right position means knowing what we need at a given time: movement or waiting, defense, or attack.

2 The six weaknesses in organizations parallel the six types of field positions because each weakness is most dangerous in a specific position. Being outmaneuvered is most dangerous in open positions, laxity in entangling positions, falling down in supporting positions, falling apart in constricted positions, disorganization in barricaded positions, and retreating in spread-out positions.

Bing-fa attributes weakness of organization solely to poor command. People are people and never the problem. A leader's decisions put the wrong organizations in bad positions at the wrong times.

¹⁰One general can command a force equal to the enemy.
Still his enemy outflanks him.
This means that his army can be outmaneuvered.

¹³Another can have strong soldiers but weak officers.
This means that his army is too lax.

¹⁵Another has strong officers but weak soldiers.
This means that his army will fall down.

¹⁷Another has subcommanders that are angry and defiant.
They attack the enemy and fight their own battles.
The commander cannot know the battlefield.
This means that his army will fall apart.

²¹Another general is weak and easygoing.
He fails to make his orders clear.
His officers and men lack direction.
This shows in his military formations.
This means that his army is disorganized.

²⁶Another general fails to predict the enemy.
He pits his small forces against larger ones.
His weak forces attack stronger ones.
He fails to pick his fights correctly.
This means that his army must retreat.

Problems with being outmaneuvered show up in unobstructed positions where free movement is possible. When we and our opponents can move easily, we must watch our relative positions.

In entangling positions we must wait until the time is right to attack. A lax organization lacks the discipline to do this.

Supportive positions result from good decision-making, but they are lost if the organization's methods fall down when challenged.

Constricted terrain demands focus. If the organization isn't united, it can't maintain a focus. This focus demands the attention and commitment of every level of the organization. If parts of the organization go in different directions, the organization falls apart.

A leader's easygoing nature and inability to make decisions is most likely to become a problem in barricaded situations. For the barricade to hold, every point must be defended against penetration. This means that every part of the organization must clearly understand its responsibilities.

Our forces are inherently weaker than our opponents' when we are in a spread-out position. Any meeting with opposition when we are in a spread-out position will force us to retreat. We should only be caught in a spread-out position if we fail to predict our opponents' actions and spread out because we think it is safe.

³¹You must know all about these six weaknesses.
You must understand the philosophies that lead to defeat.
When a general arrives, you can know what he will do.
You must study each general carefully.

You must control your field position. 3
It will always strengthen your army.

³You must predict the enemy to overpower him and win.
You must analyze the obstacles, dangers, and distances.
This is the best way to command.

⁶Understand your field position before you go to battle.
Then you will win.
You can fail to understand your field position and meet
opponents.
Then you will fail.

¹⁰You must provoke battle when you will certainly win.
It doesn't matter what you are ordered.
The government may order you not to fight.
Despite that, you must always fight when you will win.

¹⁴Sometimes provoking a battle will lead to a loss.
The government may order you to fight.
Despite that, you must avoid battle when you will lose.

These six weaknesses can appear in any situation, but they are most likely to become a problem in dealing with certain types of field positions. We can know which organizations are more suited to a given field position if we understand their weaknesses.

3 A fundamental principle of strategy is that success comes from making the right decisions about where to move.

If we know our opponents and their weaknesses, we can predict the positions they will choose. The dimensions of obstacles, dangers, and distance are the basis of our decisions.

Field position is the key in moving from one place to another, that is, advancing your position, but your field position becomes critical in times of opposition. When we are challenged, our primary responsibility is knowing the precise nature of our field position so we can know if we should defend or attack.

A mismatch of positions is like a mismatch of forces. When we are in a position of clear superiority, we must force a showdown. Even if personal or political considerations argue against a confrontation, once we recognize an opportunity, we simply have no choice.

The reverse is also true. When we are in a position of clear inferiority, we must avoid all confrontations. In making this decision, any desire for a confrontation is irrelevant.

¹⁷You must advance without desiring praise.
You must retreat without fearing shame.
The only correct move is to preserve your troops.
This is how you serve your country.
This is how you reward your nation.

Think of your soldiers as little children. 4
You can make them follow you into a deep river.
Treat them as your beloved children.
You can lead them all to their deaths.

⁵Some leaders are generous but cannot use their men.
They love their men but cannot command them.
Their men are unruly and disorganized.
These leaders create spoiled children.
Their soldiers are useless.

You may know what your soldiers will do in an attack. 5
You may not know if the enemy is vulnerable to attack.
You will then win only half the time.
You may know that the enemy is vulnerable to attack.
You may not know if your men have the capability of attack-
ing him.
You will still win only half the time.
You may know that the enemy is vulnerable to attack.
You may know that your men are ready to attack.
You may not, however, know how to position yourself in the
field for battle.
You will still win only half the time.

We don't expand into new competitive areas for egotistical reasons. Nor can we allow fear to prevent us from expanding. The dynamics of competitive environments force us to move forward or backward in response to a larger reality. This is first and foremost a matter of survival. However, it is also a matter of being successful.

4 Sun Tzu teaches that, as leaders, we must care deeply about our people. Our decisions can take them into dangerous situations fraught with change. Again, the river is Sun Tzu's symbol for change. With any authority comes tremendous responsibility.

Caring about people is more complicated than simply giving them what they want. If we truly care about people, we will do what enables their survival and success. Simply giving people what they immediately desire results in poor discipline, vague duties, bad communication, and ultimate failure.

5 In the first chapter, Sun Tzu introduced the concept of comparison (xiao) as the only path to true knowledge. At that point, we had only the five factors as the basis of comparison, but since then we have learned about unity and focus, momentum and restraint , emptiness and fullness, adaptability, and so on. All of these ideas become the basis for our knowledge about the true relative strength or power of our forces when compared with that of our opponents. However, these ideas must be joined with our understanding of the dimensions of field position to complete the strategic picture. It is equally important to understand the condition of our forces, the condition of opponents, and our relative positions. The results of our actions are the only true test for what we do or do not know.

[11]You must know how to make war.
You can then act without confusion.
You can attempt anything.

[14]We say:
Know the enemy and know yourself.
Your victory will be painless.
Know the weather and the field.
Your victory will be complete.

✦ ✦ ✦

In strategy, the equation is simple. Knowledge is the basis of competition. Knowledge makes all movement and action possible. With the right knowledge, anything is possible.

Competitive knowledge can be categorized by its effects. Knowledge about our strength relative to that of the competition determines the difficulty in achieving success. Knowledge about trends, and the ground—which includes field position—determines the completeness of our success.

Related Articles from *Sun Tzu's Playbook*

In chapter ten, Sun Tzu discusses the use of temporary positions in building relationships with voters. To learn the step-by-step techniques involved, we recommend the Sun Tzu's Art of War Playbook *articles listed below.*

2.3 Personal Interactions: making progress through personal interactions.

2.3.1 Action and Reaction: how we advance based on how others reaction to our actions.

2.3.2 Reaction Unpredictability: why we can never exactly predict the react of others.

2.3.3 Likely Reactions: the range of potential reactions in gathering information.

2.3.4 Using Questions: using questions in gathering information and predicting reactions.

4.5 Opportunity Surfaces: judging potential opportunities from a distance.

4.5.1 Surface Area: choosing opportunities on the basis of their size.

4.5.2 Surface Barriers: how to select opportunities by evaluating obstacles.

4.5.3 Surface Holding Power: sticky and slippery situations.

4.6 Six Benchmarks: simplifying the comparisons of opportunities.

4.6.1 Spread-Out Conditions: recognizing opportunities that are too large.

4.6.2 Constricted Conditions: identifying and using constricted positions.

4.6.3 Barricaded Conditions: the issues related to the extremes of obstacles.

4.6.4 Wide-Open Conditions: the issues related to an absence of barriers.

4.6.5 Fixed Conditions: positions with extreme holding power.

4.6.6 Sensitive Conditions: positions with no holding power on pursuing opportunities.

4.7 Competitive Weakness: how certain opportunities can bring out our weaknesses.

4.7.1 Command Weaknesses: the character flaws of leaders and how to exploit them.

4.7.2 Group Weaknesses: organizational weakness and where groups fail.

4.8 Climate Support: choosing new positions based on future changes.

4.9 Opportunity Mapping: two-dimensional tool for comparing opportunity probabilities.

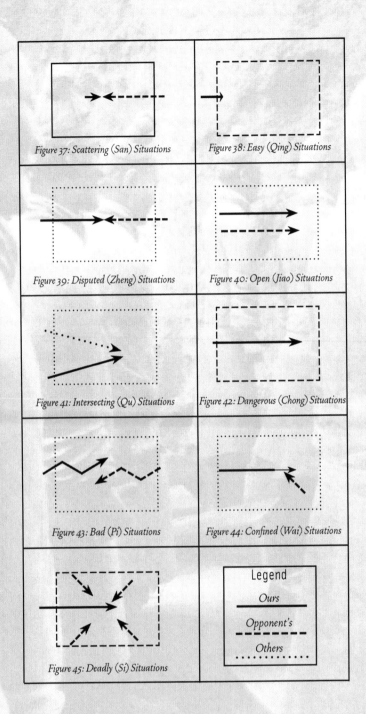

Figure 37: Scattering (San) Situations

Figure 38: Easy (Qing) Situations

Figure 39: Disputed (Zheng) Situations

Figure 40: Open (Jiao) Situations

Figure 41: Intersecting (Qu) Situations

Figure 42: Dangerous (Chong) Situations

Figure 43: Bad (Pi) Situations

Figure 44: Confined (Wai) Situations

Figure 45: Deadly (Si) Situations

Legend

Ours

Opponent's

Others

Chapter 11

Types of Terrain: Reacting to Situations

The term "terrain" or "ground" (*di*) used here also means "situation." This chapter describes nine dynamic situations that arise during a competitive campaign. These situations are defined by three factors: the position of our forces, the position of opposing forces, and the nature of the ground. These situations are dynamic because forces move, changing the situation as the ground changes. For each situation, *bing-fa* prescribes one correct reaction.

These nine dynamic situations can be shown graphically as a series of diagrams similar to force vectors. We show these diagrams on the facing page (*Figures 37-45*).

The center of each diagram is the terrain, which is shown as a rectangle. The terrain can belong to us (shown with solid lines) or our opponents (dashes), or it can be neutral (dotted lines). The ground can have certain characteristics that restrict or allow passage in different areas. Though these conditions are not shown directly on our diagrams, they are represented by the type of movement allowed.

The movement of the relevant forces is shown with arrows. Arrows represent our forces (solid arrows), our opponent's forces (dashes), and other forces (dotted). In most situations, the nature of the ground determines the relationship of these forces and their movement, which is largely the point of this chapter. In some circumstances, the movement, position, and relationship of forces determines the situation on the ground.

Types of Terrain

SUN TZU SAID:

Use the art of war. 1
Know when the terrain will scatter you.
Know when the terrain is easy.
Know when the terrain is disputed.
Know when the terrain is open.
Know when the terrain is intersecting.
Know when the terrain is dangerous.
Know when the terrain is bad.
Know when the terrain is confined.
Know when the terrain is deadly.

11Warring parties must sometimes fight inside their own
territory.
This is scattering terrain.

13When you enter hostile territory, your penetration is shallow.
This is easy terrain.

15Some terrain gives you an advantageous position.
But it gives others an advantageous position as well.
This is disputed terrain.

Reacting to Situations

1 Though some of the English terms for the "nine grounds" may look familiar, the Chinese terms are unique. The first, *san*, means "scattered" or "diffuse." The next, *qing*, means "easy," "light," or "simple." The next, *zheng*, which we already know as "conflict" also means "to quarrel." The next, *jiao*, (open), means literally "to cross," or "to join." The next, *qu*, means "to intersect" or "highway." The next, *chong* (dangerous), means literally "heavy" or "serious." The next, *pi* (bad), means literally "ruined" or "destroyed." The next, *wai* (confined), means "to encircle," or "to surround." The last, *si*, means "to die" or "extremity."

In describing scattering (*san*) terrain, the sense is that different leaders must sometimes battle for their own territory. In other words, in this situation, our opponent challenges us for our territory.

The idea of easy (*qing*) terrain is that when we first move into an opponent's arena, we make easy progress, at least at first.

We enter into another situation when we go after an area that is obviously desirable to opposing parties. This creates conflict (*zheng*), which *bing-fa* teaches is inherently costly in competition.

¹⁸You can use some terrain to advance easily.
Others can advance along with you.
This is open terrain.

²¹Everyone shares access to a given area.
The first one to arrive there can gather a larger group than
anyone else.
This is intersecting terrain.

²⁴You can penetrate deeply into hostile territory.
Then many hostile cities are behind you.
This is dangerous terrain.

²⁷There are mountain forests.
There are dangerous obstructions.
There are reservoirs.
Everyone confronts these obstacles on a campaign.
They make bad terrain.

³²In some areas, the entry passage is narrow.
You are closed in as you try to get out of them.
In this type of area, a few people can effectively attack your
much larger force.
This is confined terrain.

³⁶You can sometimes survive only if you fight quickly.
You will die if you delay.
This is deadly terrain.

Another translation for *jiao* is "crossing," which avoids the confusion with *tong* (open), the idea of unobstructed. The concept *jiao* means crossing an open area in a race with opponents.

Qu, or intersecting terrain, is accessible to different non-competing groups. It makes it possible to unite with these groups to form alliances. Not all other organizations are potential competitors; some are allies that can work with us to develop an opportunity.

Chong terrain is dangerous only because when we penetrate deeply into an opposing territory, we are dependent on the success of our campaign since we are cut off from the source of our resources.

Pi (bad) terrains or situations are dangerously obstructed (*xian*). Though useful for defense as barricaded ground, in dynamic situations they make progress or movement (*hang*) exceedingly difficult. All campaigns will include necessary passages through difficult areas, during which we must deal with obstructions.

Similarly, w*ai* (confined) situations are different from the constricted (*ai*) positions in the last chapter. These situations are a transitional constraint. During the transition, a few people or resources are the key to success. Because we must rely upon a few people, those people are vulnerable to attack by the opposition.

Si (deadly or desperate) situations are the most dynamic of all. With each passing moment, we grow weaker while the opposition grows stronger. In these situations, if we hesitate we are lost.

39To be successful, you must control scattering terrain by avoiding battle.
Control easy terrain by not stopping.
Control disputed terrain by not attacking.
Control open terrain by staying with the enemy's forces.
Control intersecting terrain by uniting with your allies.
Control dangerous terrain by plundering.
Control bad terrain by keeping on the move.
Control confined terrain by using surprise.
Control deadly terrain by fighting.

Go to an area that is known to be good for waging war. 2
Use it to cut off the enemy's contact between his front and back lines.
Prevent his small parties from relying on his larger force.
Stop his strong divisions from rescuing his weak ones.
Prevent his officers from getting their men together.
Chase his soldiers apart to stop them from amassing.
Harass them to prevent their ranks from forming.

8When joining battle gives you an advantage, you must do it.
When it isn't to your benefit, you must avoid it.

10A daring soldier may ask:
"A large, organized enemy army and its general are coming.
What do I do to prepare for them?"

As we navigate each of these situations, the challenge is maintaining control. Strategically, control is what prevents a situation from degrading into chaos. For each situation, there is only one correct response that maintains control. For example, in scattering situations, the response that maintains control is avoiding battle. In easy situations, the response that maintains control is avoid stopping, and so on. Each response remains our standing orders until the situation changes. The situation changes as another situation develops to replace it. Campaigns are dynamic as they shift from one situation to another.

2 The lesson in dividing the enemy addresses the issue of scattering terrain. We don't want our opponents to attack us on our own ground because these attacks scatter our forces. Instead, we want to take the battle to our opponents, putting them on scattering ground. On their own ground, local divisions also naturally divide them. Attacking opponents on their ground means forcing them to address our challenge to their unity or completeness, forcing them to lose their focus, and dividing their ability to organize.

If we are attacked on our own ground, we avoid the battle. When we can take the battle to the opponent's ground, we should do it.

The question is, how do we avoid the battle when a capable opponent is coming into our territory? The basic prescription of "don't fight" is more difficult than it seems.

¹³Tell him:
"First seize an area that the enemy must have.
Then he will pay attention to you.
Mastering speed is the essence of war.
Take advantage of a large enemy's inability to keep up.
Use a philosophy of avoiding difficult situations.
Attack the area where he doesn't expect you."

You must use the philosophy of an invader. 3
Invade deeply and then concentrate your forces.
This controls your men without oppressing them.

⁴Get your supplies from the riches of the territory.
They are sufficient to supply your whole army.

⁶Take care of your men and do not overtax them.
Your esprit de corps increases your momentum.
Keep your army moving and plan for surprises.
Make it difficult for the enemy to count your forces.
Position your men where there is no place to run.
They will then face death without fleeing.
They will find a way to survive.
Your officers and men will fight to their utmost.

¹⁴Military officers who are committed lose their fear.
When they have nowhere to run, they must stand firm.
Deep in enemy territory, they are captives.
Since they cannot escape, they will fight.

The only way to prevent opponents from coming into our area is by quickly taking the battle to them. When Sun Tzu says that we want our opponents to "pay attention to us," he means that they will then have to deal with our advance into their territory instead of advancing into ours. Such a preemptive strike isn't a true advance, where we expect to hold the ground. We don't actually want to confront our opponents; we want to harass and disorganize them.

3 An invasion scatters the forces of those invaded, but it has the opposite effect on the forces of the invader (*ke*). When we are deep in unknown territory we tend to come together and focus.

Invasions are dangerous situations in which the challenge is getting resources, which we must get by plunder.

These dangerous situations, as invasions, have a powerful positive emotional effect on people. We must be cautious about our people's mental condition when we are invading new areas. This means moving people carefully and keeping our opponents ignorant of our plans. However, taking care of our forces doesn't necessarily mean avoiding challenges. Indeed, do-or-die situations are the ultimate challenge; we trust our people to rise to the challenge in order to survive.

Once we and our people are completely committed to the project, we will find a way to make it work. Sun Tzu describes us as captives of the dangerous situations when we are deeply committed in a hostile territory.

18Commit your men completely.
Without being posted, they will be on guard.
Without being asked, they will get what is needed.
Without being forced, they will be dedicated.
Without being given orders, they can be trusted.

23Stop them from guessing by removing all their doubts.
Stop them from dying by giving them no place to run.

25Your officers may not be rich.
Nevertheless, they still desire plunder.
They may die young.
Nevertheless, they still want to live forever.

29You must order the time of attack.
Officers and men may sit and weep until their lapels are wet.
When they stand up, tears may stream down their cheeks.
Put them in a position where they cannot run.
They will show the greatest courage under fire.

Make good use of war. 4
This demands instant reflexes.
You must develop these instant reflexes.
Act like an ordinary mountain snake.
If people strike your head then stop them with your tail.
If they strike your tail then stop them with your head.
If they strike your middle then use both your head and tail.

Bing-fa teaches us to have a tremendous faith in the strength and intelligence of individuals when their self-interest is on the line. When people are completely committed to a cause and dependent on its success, they don't have to be managed. They are capable of managing themselves and doing whatever is necessary.

The secret to giving people responsibility is keeping them completely informed about the seriousness of their situation.

Each of us has an inner entrepreneur who desires wealth. We will take risks to be successful because we desire more than what we have. This is why the secret of dangerous situations is plunder, which offers riches, which minimizes fear.

When we challenge ourselves and others, we can all rise to extraordinary heights. This doesn't mean that we won't have serious fears, especially as the moment of danger approaches. When we are afraid or uncertain, the secret to overcoming our fears is total commitment such that we have no choice but to act.

4 As we move from one competitive situation to another, our entire organization must instantly recognize our situation and react appropriately. Ignorance and poor communication prevent different parts of the organization from supporting each other. In competitive situations, every part of our organization must be able to independently synchronize reactions based upon our shared knowledge of our situation and the appropriate response.

[8]A daring soldier asks:
"Can any army imitate these instant reflexes?"
We answer:
"It can."

[12]To command and get the most out of proud people, you
must study adversity.
People work together when they are in the same boat during
a storm.
In this situation, one rescues the other just as the right
hand helps the left.

[15]Use adversity correctly.
Tether your horses and bury your wagon's wheels.
Still, you can't depend on this alone.
An organized force is braver than lone individuals.
This is the art of organization.
Put the tough and weak together.
You must also use the terrain.

[22]Make good use of war.
Unite your men as one.
Never let them give up.

The commander must be a military professional. 5
This requires confidence and detachment.
You must maintain dignity and order.
You must control what your men see and hear.
They must follow you without knowing your plans.

Many leaders don't trust the ability of their people to make independent decisions correctly and quickly. We must train our people so that we can depend upon their reactions as new situations and new challenges arise.

"Proud" is an interesting term because the character used (*wu*, "to boast") is also the name of the ancient kingdom, *Wu*, for which the original *Art of War* was written. The message is that we must put our people into dangerous or even deadly situations to get them working together. Everyone's success must depend on the success of the organization (or kingdom) as a whole.

The concept of organization is expressed as a Chinese character that means government or political affairs, but the radicals of this character mean "to correct by striking"—in other words, the use of coercion or discipline. However, Sun Tzu does not use the force of authority to punish, but rather to group people and position them properly. People must work together in a way that minimizes their weaknesses and leverages their strengths.

Many situations in a competitive campaign are dangerous, bad, and even deadly, but they can draw people together and strengthen them if we govern them correctly.

5 Leaders are separate from the organization. A leader cannot be "just one of the guys." People want and need to look up to and respect their leaders. This means that we, if we want to lead, must act in a way that inspires devotion. We must manage everything that we do and say considering its emotional effect on people.

^{6}You can reinvent your men's roles.

You can change your plans.

You can use your men without their understanding.

^{9}You must shift your campgrounds.

You must take detours from the ordinary routes.

You must use your men without giving them your strategy.

^{12}A commander provides what is needed now.

This is like climbing high and being willing to kick away your ladder.

You must be able to lead your men deeply into different surrounding territory.

And yet, you can discover the opportunity to win.

^{16}You must drive men like a flock of sheep.

You must drive them to march.

You must drive them to attack.

You must never let them know where you are headed.

You must unite them into a great army.

You must then drive them against all opposition.

This is the job of a true commander.

^{23}You must adapt to the different terrain.

You must adapt to find an advantage.

You must manage your people's affections.

You must study all these skills.

If we and our people understand the shared goal and shared danger, we aren't tied to the specifics of the current plan, which, many times, may lead to difficulty and dangers.

People who are habituated to their jobs lose sight of their goals. We must continually make detours to stay challenged, but we cannot divulge our plans when planning a dangerous movement.

A leader must understand both the future and the present. Vision (*jian*) gives us the ability to see what is possible in the future, but our job as managers is to focus on addressing the needs of the moment. We may at times choose to put ourselves and others into challenging situations so that we can rise to our full potential and uncover true opportunities.

The term *keui* that Sun Tzu uses for "drive" means simultaneously to "drive a carriage," "spur a horse," and "drive out." The idea is not slave driving, but guiding, inspiring, and getting people out of their comfortable roles. The more general idea is to get them moving. They must leave where they don't want to leave and go where they don't want to go. We use drive specifically to overcome obstacles, translated here as "opposition."

The rules of adaptability or change require that we adjust our behavior to the situation or terrain. Sun Tzu uses another term for "situation," *ching*, that has a second meaning of "feelings," or "affection," to reflect a parallel between managing the two.

Always use the philosophy of invasion. 6
Deep invasions concentrate your forces.
Shallow invasions scatter your forces.
When you leave your country and cross the border, you must
take control.
This is always critical ground.
You can sometimes move in any direction.
This is always intersecting ground.
You can penetrate deeply into a territory.
This is always dangerous ground.
You penetrate only a little way.
This is always easy ground.
Your retreat is closed and the path ahead tight.
This is always confined ground.
There is sometimes no place to run.
This is always deadly ground.

[16]To use scattering terrain correctly, you must inspire your
men's devotion.
On easy terrain, you must keep in close communication.
On disputed terrain, you try to hamper the enemy's progress.
On open terrain, you must carefully defend your chosen position.
On intersecting terrain, you must solidify your alliances.
On dangerous terrain, you must ensure your food supplies.
On bad terrain, you must keep advancing along the road.
On confined terrain, you must stop information leaks from
your headquarters.
On deadly terrain, you must show what you can do by
killing the enemy.

6 We describe these terrains as situations because Sun Tzu wants us to see a competitive campaign as a process that has a beginning, a middle, and an end. At the beginning we must have a "philosophy of invasion," that is, we compete by taking the battle to our opponents instead of waiting for an attack and having our forces scattered. *Ke* or invasion is a philosophy of expansion and growth. In this expansion, certain situations are likely to occur. At first, progress is easy. Then we are faced with the options of intersecting ground—shared situations in which we can choose allies. As time goes on, we make progress, but the going gets more difficult. This is a dangerous situation. For Sun Tzu it is axiomatic that if the situations are easy, we haven't made much progress, but if they are difficult, we are making progress. Progress will eventually limit our options, creating confined situations. In the end, however, it always comes down to the need to do or die, when we must prove what we can do.

In every situation, we must use psychology as well as action. In scattering situations, devotion unites the organization. In easy situations, communication keeps the organization moving. In disputed situations, we can't attack opponents, but we can harass them. In open situations, we must be cautious because opponents can move on us. In intersecting situations, we have to strengthen the alliances we make. In dangerous situations, we don't want to worry about our source of supply. Food is important because it sends a message. In bad situations, we need to follow the easiest path available. In confined situations, where we must keep our circumstances a secret, we must prevent leaks. In do-or-die situations, we must fight to destroy our opponents.

²⁵Make your men feel like an army.
Surround them and they will defend themselves.
If they cannot avoid it, they will fight.
If they are under pressure, they will obey.

Do the right thing when you don't know your 7
different enemies' plans.
Don't attempt to meet them.

³You don't know the position of mountain forests, dangerous
obstructions, and reservoirs?
Then you cannot march the army.
You don't have local guides?
You won't get any of the benefits of the terrain.

⁷There are many factors in war.
You may lack knowledge of any one of them.
If so, it is wrong to take a nation into war.

¹⁰You must be able to control your government's war.
If you divide a big nation, it will be unable to put together a
large force.
Increase your enemy's fear of your ability.
Prevent his forces from getting together and organizing.

In the end, we win the dedication of our people by putting them in situations in which they can win and, just as importantly, must win. If we leave our people a way out, we are inviting eventual failure. We must use situations to create total commitment.

7 Sun Tzu sees these nine situations in the context of knowledge, vision, movement, and positioning. To be successful in a campaign, we must use vision to see an opening in our opponent's plans.

Vision comes from knowledge of the territory. We cannot see an opportunity worthy of a campaign unless we have an understanding of the area in which we are operating. Without knowledge and the resulting vision, we cannot move or use positioning to get the benefit of the situation on the ground.

Though all four skills—knowledge, vision, movement, and positioning—are necessary, knowledge is the key to everything. Without knowing what we are doing, we cannot be successful.

The four skills determine our progress in a given situation, but the fifth key to success is unity. If we can divide our opponent's forces while keeping our forces united and focused, our ability to take advantage of a situation becomes more certain. Division works both physically and as an emotional and psychological tool.

14Do the right thing and do not arrange outside alliances
before their time.
You will not have to assert your authority prematurely.
Trust only yourself and your self-interest.
This increases the enemy's fear of you.
You can make one of his allies withdraw.
His whole nation can fall.

20Distribute rewards without worrying about having a system.
Halt without the government's command.
Attack with the whole strength of your army.
Use your army as if it were a single man.

24Attack with skill.
Do not discuss it.
Attack when you have an advantage.
Do not talk about the dangers.
When you can launch your army into deadly ground, even if
it stumbles, it can still survive.
You can be weakened in a deadly battle and yet be stronger
afterward.

30Even a large force can fall into misfortune.
If you fall behind, however, you can still turn defeat into victory.
You must use the skills of war.
To survive, you must adapt yourself to your enemy's purpose.
You must stay with him no matter where he goes.
It may take a thousand miles to kill the general.
If you correctly understand him, you can find the skill to do it.

In the realm of unity, Sun Tzu is deeply suspicious of alliances that don't happen naturally—that is, those for which we have to compete. Though everything is a competition, unity is so important and so difficult between organizations that all alliances are suspect. Add to this the idea that large organizations are inherently slower than small ones, and alliances become even more difficult to justify. Sun Tzu teaches us to make war on alliances rather than depend on them.

One of the most important advantages of working outside alliances is that we don't have to deal with the politics of larger organizations. We can distribute rewards, eliminate unnecessary programs, focus our resources, and enjoy the general benefits of unity.

Our ability to attack—that is, take over a new position— depends on our skills. Since skill depends on knowledge (*zhi*), we keep our opponents ignorant of our plans. We also keep our people unaware of the dangers to keep them focused on the task at hand. We use the dangers of do-or-die (*si*) situations to purposefully focus our abilities on the task at hand. Though do-or-die situations are inherently difficult, we can meet the problems that they present and become more powerful for that experience.

The larger reality is that, especially when it comes to exploring new areas, we can fail. However, a central precept of *bing-fa* is that we manage and limit our potential failures so that we can recover from them. Normally, we do this by keeping our movements small and local. This limits our potential losses, but even a large failure is not a death sentence. Nor are distant campaigns inherently unsuccessful. Knowledge of our situation is the true key to our success.

Manage your government correctly at the start of a war. 8
Close your borders and tear up passports.
Block the passage of envoys.
Encourage the halls of power to rise to the occasion.
You must use any means to put an end to politics.
Your enemy's people will leave you an opening.
You must instantly invade through it.

8Immediately seize a place that they love.
Do it quickly.
Trample any border to pursue the enemy.
Use your judgment about when to fight.

12Doing the right thing at the start of war is like
approaching a woman.
Your enemy's men must open the door.
After that, you should act like a streaking rabbit.
The enemy will be unable to catch you.

♦ ♦ ♦

8 When we plan to undertake a competitive campaign, we must know what we are doing. First, we must get control of information and make sure that information about our plans doesn't get to our opponents. We discourage internal politics because political considerations are inherently divisive. We then wait to see an opening or weakness. When we see that opening, we use the philosophy of the invader to move through it.

A successful competitive campaign depends on winning a quick success, ideally one that emotionally hurts our opponents. We must act quickly to segment the market or trample a border. We must look for support from the trends of the moment.

Even though Sun Tzu provides a detailed vision of how competitive systems work, he also teaches that success is an art as well as a science. Using Sun Tzu's strategy demands the subtlety and sensitivity of a man wooing a woman. This is especially true in understanding the subtleties of the nine situations we face. We have to await the right opportunity. Then our reaction demands pure speed.

Related Articles from *Sun Tzu's Playbook*

In chapter eleven, Sun Tzu explains instant situation response. To learn the step-by-step techniques involved, we recommend the Sun Tzu's Art of War Playbook *articles listed below.*

6.0 Situation Response: selecting the actions most appropriate to a situation.

6.1 Situation Recognition: situation recognition in making advances.

6.1.1 Conditioned Reflexes: how we develop automatic, instantaneous responses.

6.1.2 Prioritizing Conditions: parsing complex competitive conditions into simple responses.

6.2 Campaign Evaluation: how we justify continued investment in an ongoing campaign.

6.2.1 Campaign Flow: seeing campaigns as a series of situations that flow logically from one to another.

6.2.2 Campaign Goals: assessing the value of a campaign by a larger mission.

6.3 Campaign Patterns: how knowing campaign stages gives us insight into our situation.

6.3.1 Early-Stage Situations: the common situations that arise the earliest in campaigns.

6.3.2 Middle-Stage Situations: how progress creates transitional situations in campaigns.

6.3.3 Late-Stage Situations: understanding the final and most dangerous stages of campaigns.

6.4 Nine Situations: the nine common competitive situations.

6.4.1 Dissipating Situations: situations where defensive unity is destroyed.

6.4.2 Easy Situations: recognizing situations of easy initial progress.

6.4.3 Contentious Situations: identifying situations that invite conflict.

6.4.4 Open Situations: recognizing situations that are races without a course.

6.4.5 Intersecting Situations: recognizing situations that bring people together.

6.4.6 Serious Situations: identifying situations where resources can be cut off.

6.4.7 Difficult Situations: recognizing situations where serious barriers must be overcome.

6.4.8 Limited Situations: identifying situations defined by a bottleneck.

6.4.9 Desperate Situations: identifying situations where destruction is possible.

6.5 Nine Responses: using the best responses to the nine common competitive situations.

6.5.1 Dissipating Response: responding to dissipation by the use of offense as defense.

6.5.2 Easy Response: responding to easy situations by overcoming complacency.

6.5.3 Contentious Response: responding to contentious situations by knowing how to avoid conflict.

6.5.4 Open Response: responding to open situations by keeping up with the opposition.

6.5.5 Intersecting Response: the formation of situational alliances.

6.5.6 Serious Response: responding to serious situations by finding immediate income.

6.5.7 Difficult Response: the role of persistence in responding to difficult situations.

6.5.8 Limited Response: the need for secret speed in limited situations.

6.5.9 Desperate Response: using all our resources in responding to desperate situations.

6.6 Campaign Pause: knowing when to stop advancing a position.

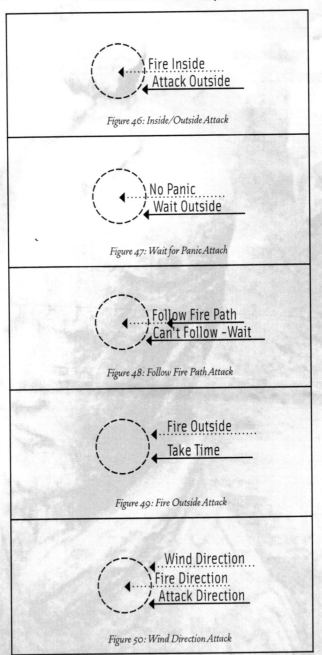

Figure 46: Inside/Outside Attack

Figure 47: Wait for Panic Attach

Figure 48: Follow Fire Path Attack

Figure 49: Fire Outside Attack

Figure 50: Wind Direction Attack

Chapter 12

Attacking with Fire: Using the Environment

Although Sun Tzu uses this chapter to cover a specific weapon, fire, its broader subject is using any weapon, with an emphasis on leveraging forces in the environment as weapons. Fire (*huo*) is a useful analogy for broad, indiscriminate attacks. Like many such weapons, fire is a danger both to the target and to the attacker. Sun Tzu uses the Chinese term *gong*, translated as "attack," in many ways. Sometimes, he means moving into new areas, other, hampering opponents. Here, he means attacking opponents with a weapon.

Fire is an environmental weapon. We can only start a fire if the conditions in the environment—that is, on the ground and in heaven—support it. So we must choose the proper ground for fire attacks. More importantly, we don't control fire once it is started. Its direction, speed, and duration depend on factors of climate, which are beyond our control, but which we can observe.

In describing environmental attacks, Sun Tzu identifies five different targets for these attacks. Though enumerated as targets for fire, they illustrate the five categories of targets for attack by any type of weapon. These five targets are listed in priority from the least important to the most important.

The most important aspects of environmental attacks are how we follow up if we are attacking, or how we respond if we are attacked. Sun Tzu offers five approaches that depend on how the fire attack is waged and the situations that develop from the attack (*Figures 46-50*).

Attacking with Fire

Sᴜɴ Tᴢᴜ sᴀɪᴅ:

There are five ways of attacking with fire. 1
The first is burning troops.
The second is burning supplies.
The third is burning supply transport.
The fourth is burning storehouses.
The fifth is burning camps.

7To make fire, you must have the resources.
To build a fire, you must prepare the raw materials.

9To attack with fire, you must be in the right season.
To start a fire, you must have the time.

11Choose the right season.
The weather must be dry.

13Choose the right time.
Pick a season when the grass is as high as the side of a cart.

15You can tell the proper days by the stars in the night sky.
You want days when the wind rises in the morning.

Using the Environment

1 In giving us the targets for attacking with fire, Sun Tzu is also giving us the priorities for attacking in general. First are people (*ren*). Next, in keeping with *bing-fa*'s economic focus, are supplies (*ji*), literally stores or savings. Next is the transportation of supplies (*zi*). Next is storehouses (*ku*). Finally, we have camps, literally groupings (*dui*). Each of these is a focal point for an attack.

To use a fire attack, the ground must provide the raw materials. So fire is a metaphor for all opportunities, since we don't create them.

This attack, and all others, also depends on heaven and the climate, which means we must discover a window of opportunity.

Environmental attacks in general include using publicity, lawsuits, regulations, and so on, which all depend on outside trends.

We can create neither the fuel nor the right climate for these attacks; we must wait until the right conditions present themselves.

We can, however, observe the conditions developing to support these types of attacks and choose a time when forces support them.

Everyone attacks with fire. 2

You must create five different situations with fire and be able
to adjust to them.

3You start a fire inside the enemy's camp.
Then attack the enemy's periphery.

5You launch a fire attack, but the enemy remains calm.
Wait and do not attack.

7The fire reaches its height.
Follow its path if you can.
If you can't follow it, stay where you are.

10Spreading fires on the outside of camp can kill.
You can't always get fire inside the enemy's camp.
Take your time in spreading it.

13Set the fire when the wind is at your back.
Don't attack into the wind.
Daytime winds last a long time.
Night winds fade quickly.

17Every army must know how to adjust to the five possible
attacks by fire.
Use many men to guard against them.

2 Everyone can leverage the environment when an opportunity presents itself, so we must be prepared for both defense and offense. This means recognizing five different possible attack scenarios.

First, if the environmental attack threatens the inside or core of an opponent, then our forces pressure the outside.

If the target doesn't panic, the second approach is simply to wait for the fire to do its damage without attacking directly.

Third, environmental fires build and then, unavoidably, fade with time. When the heat of the fire fades, we can follow the weaknesses or openings that it creates in our opponent.

The fourth situation is an indirect attack, working from the outside to the inside. This type of attack takes more time and patience to wait for it to work.

The fifth situation is to leverage the pressures or fashions—*weng* means both "wind" and "fashion"—in the environment. If certain types of news stories, lawsuits, or regulations are popular, they are more like to be used as attacks.

We must constantly evaluate the environment to identify the opportunities for environmental attacks. We need to have people focused on developing them and protecting us against them.

When you use fire to assist your attacks, you are clever. 3
Water can add force to an attack.
You can also use water to disrupt an enemy's forces.
It does not, however, take his resources.

You win in battle by getting the opportunity to attack. 4
It is dangerous if you fail to study how to accomplish this
achievement.
As commander, you cannot waste your opportunities.

4We say:
A wise leader plans success.
A good general studies it.
If there is little to be gained, don't act.
If there is little to win, do not use your men.
If there is no danger, don't fight.

10As the leader, you cannot let your anger interfere with the
success of your forces.
As commander, you cannot let yourself become enraged
before you go to battle.
Join the battle only when it is in your advantage to act.
If there is no advantage in joining a battle, stay put.

14Anger can change back into happiness.
Rage can change back into joy.
A nation once destroyed cannot be brought back to life.
Dead men do not return to the living.

3 Sun Tzu contrasts attacks where we initiate the heat on our opponents with another category of environmental attack. Water is Sun Tzu's metaphor for change. Changes, such as technological change, put pressure on opponents, but they aren't as damaging.

4 Many people are uncomfortable using environmental attacks against their opponents. However, like all competitive tools that we have, we must make the most of these attacks when an opportunity presents itself. We cannot afford to disregard them.

These attacks (and all competitive attacks) require the proper foresight and deliberation on the part of the leader. They should not be used lightly. Remember the lessons of chapter 2: attacking is always costly; even these fire attacks have costs. We must make sure that we have something real to gain before we undertake them. Victory, defined in Sun Tzu's terms, is making winning pay!

Here, Sun Tzu uses fire as a metaphor for emotion. Environmental attacks should not be used just for emotional reasons whenever an opportunity presents itself. Sun Tzu defines "opportunity" not just as the opportunity to move forward, but the opportunity to win stronger position. Using any attack without the opportunity of winning a clear advantage is simply too risky.

Bing-fa teaches us that emotions are fleeting—as we have said before—belonging to the realm of heaven, where everything changes. We must control our emotions since the effects of our emotions have life-and-death consequences.

[18]This fact must make a wise leader cautious.
A good general is on guard.

[20]Your philosophy must be to keep the nation peaceful and
the army intact.

❖ ❖ ❖

We cannot be too sensitive to use these attacks, but we must never use them out of anger, and we must always defend against them.

Our mission must be productive in the sense of enriching the organization so that we preserve and build our competitive ability.

♦ ♦ ♦

Related Articles from *Sun Tzu's Playbook*

In chapter twelve, Sun Tzu discusses the use of environmental weapons. To learn the step-by-step techniques involved, we recommend the Sun Tzu's Art of War Playbook *articles listed below.*

9.0 Understanding Vulnerability: the use of common environmental attacks.

9.1 Climate Vulnerability: our vulnerability to environmental crises arising from change.

9.1.1 Climate Rivals: how changing conditions create opponents.

9.1.2 Threat Development: how changing conditions create environmental threats.

9.2 Points of Vulnerability: our points of vulnerability during an environmental crisis.

9.2.1 Personnel Risk: the vulnerability of key individuals.

9.2.2 Immediate Resource Risk: the vulnerability of the resources required for immediate use.

9.2.3 Transportation/Communication Risk: how firestorms choke normal channels of movement and communication.

9.2.4 Asset Risk: the threats to our fixed assets.

9.2.5 Organizational Risk: targeting the roles and responsibilities within an organization.

9.3 Crisis Leadership: maintaining the support of our supporters during attacks.

9.3.1 Mutual Danger: how we use mutual danger to create mutual strength.

9.3.2 Message Control: communication methods to use during a crisis.

9.4 Crisis Defense: how vulnerabilities are exploited and defended during a crisis.

9.4.1 Division Defense: preventing organizational division during a crisis.

9.4.2 Panic Defense: preventing the mistakes arising from panic during a crisis.

9.4.3 Defending Openings: how to defend openings created by a crisis.

9.4.4 Defending Alliances: dealing with guilt by association.

9.4.5 Defensive Balance: using short-term conditions to tip the balance in a crisis.

9.5 Crisis Exploitation: how to successfully use an opponent's crisis.

9.5.1 Adversarial Opportunities: how our opponents' crises can create opportunities.

9.5.2 Avoiding Emotion: the danger of exploiting environmental vulnerabilities for purely emotion reasons.

9.6 Constant Vigilance: where to focus our attention to preserve our positions.

Five Information Conduits

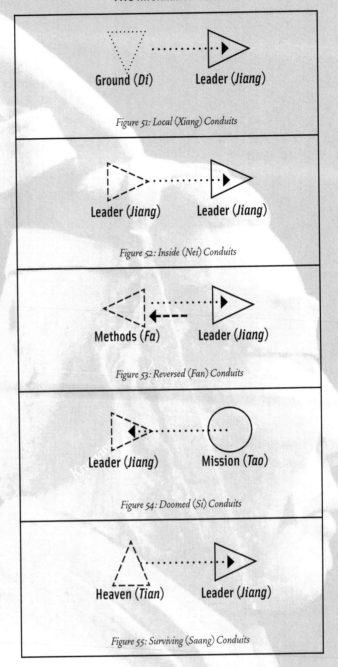

Ground (*Di*) Leader (*Jiang*)

Figure 51: Local (Xiang) Conduits

Leader (*Jiang*) Leader (*Jiang*)

Figure 52: Inside (Nei) Conduits

Methods (*Fa*) Leader (*Jiang*)

Figure 53: Reversed (Fan) Conduits

Leader (*Jiang*) Mission (*Tao*)

Figure 54: Doomed (Si) Conduits

Heaven (*Tian*) Leader (*Jiang*)

Figure 55: Surviving (Saang) Conduits

Chapter 13

用 間

Using Spies: Using Information

The final topic of Sun Tzu's *Bing-Fa* is the flow of information. Classical strategy teaches that the flow of information is the most important element of creating a successful strategy. His view of the importance of information arises naturally from his economic view of competition. In his view, since we must pay a great deal to move men and materials, we are wise to pay a little to know how to place those resources more accurately.

Sun Tzu offers five different categories of information flow. Each category ties directly to one of the five key elements—mission, climate, ground, leader, and methods—with which we began the book.

Like the movement of forces over land, the flow of information can be charted. We illustrate the five categories of information flow (*Figures 51-55*) using our standard symbols for the key elements. As in our other diagrams, solid lines represent our elements, dashed lines represent opponents, and dotted lines represent neutral components.

Notice that there are four information flows that bring information into our organization and only one that broadcasts information. And in that one, the main purpose of communication is to use *gui*, that is, deception or illusion, to shape the perceptions of others. Spreading our mission to potential allies is also a potential use of this type of information conduit.

Using Spies

SUN TZU SAID:

All successful armies require thousands of men. 1
They invade and march thousands of miles.
Whole families are destroyed.
Other families must be heavily taxed.
Every day, a large amount of money must be spent.

⁶Internal and external events force people to move.
They are unable to work while on the road.
They are unable to find and hold a useful job.
This affects 70 percent of thousands of families.

¹⁰You can watch and guard for years.
Then a single battle can determine victory in a day.
Despite this, bureaucrats worship the value of their salary
money too dearly.
They remain ignorant of the enemy's condition.
The result is cruel.

¹⁵They are not leaders of men.
They are not servants of the state.
They are not masters of victory.

Using Information

1 This chapter is about information, but it begins by talking about the costs of competition. It raises many of the exact same issues that were raised earlier in chapter two. Competition is costly. Its costs take resources from the productive part of the organization. We must compete, and we must control costs.

The problem of cost is multiplied by its negative impact on productivity. Competition is disruptive. The changes resulting from competition make it difficult to do productive work. This is even truer in economic competition where work depends on sales.

Increasing productivity is a gradual process, but success or failure in competition is not predictable. After long periods of stasis, a single decisive event can change everything overnight. Because of the "tipping point" nature of competition, nothing is more critical than having the right information at the right time. Because of these economics, knowledge is always worth money.

Sun Tzu teaches frugality in every other area of competition, with the idea that we increase our chances of financial success by keeping our costs low. This thinking, however, does not apply to information.

[18]You need a creative leader and a worthy commander.
You must move your troops to the right places to beat others.
You must accomplish your attack and escape unharmed.
This requires foreknowledge.
You can obtain foreknowledge.
You can't get it from demons or spirits.
You can't see it from professional experience.
You can't check it with analysis.
You can only get it from other people.
You must always know the enemy's situation.

You must use five types of spies. 2
You need local spies.
You need inside spies.
You need double agents.
You need doomed spies.
You need surviving spies.

[7]You need all five types of spies.
No one must discover your methods.
You will then be able to put together a true picture.
This is the commander's most valuable resource.

[11]You need local spies.
Get them by hiring people from the countryside.

[13]You need inside spies.
Win them by subverting government officials.

There are two critical and central ideas here. First, it is timely information and timely information alone that makes our decisions effective. The process of *bing-fa* creates success only if based on timely information. Second, all timely information comes from human intelligence, that is, knowing what others are planning. All our experience and all the data in our computers are reflections of the past, not the future. Forecasting works only for productive systems. The chaos of competition is not predictable in the same way. Only human beings can tell us what is planned for the future. In competition, we depend on other people for timely information.

2. Though translated as "spies," the Chinese character Sun Tzu used, *gaan*, actually means "a space between," that is, a go-between, a conduit of information, specifically a conduit of planned moves. *Xiang gaan* are local or village conduits. *Nei gaan* are inside or internal conduits. *Fan gaan* are reverse or flipped conduits. *Si gaan* are dead conduits. *Saang gaan* are newly born or fresh conduits.

All five types of information sources are necessary to put together a complete picture of the future. For this to work, we must keep our information sources a secret. Otherwise, people will naturally change their plans.

Local spies provide current information about a given area, that is, the contested ground.

Inside spies are those close to decision-makers who can report on the plans of our allies, opponents, or customers.

¹⁵You need double agents.
Discover enemy agents and convert them.

¹⁷You need doomed spies.
Deceive professionals into being captured.
Let them know your orders.
They then take those orders to your enemy.

²¹You need surviving spies.
Someone must return with a report.

Your job is to build a complete army. 3
No relations are as intimate as the ones with spies.
No rewards are too generous for spies.
No work is as secret as that of spies.

⁵If you aren't clever and wise, you can't use spies.
If you aren't fair and just, you can't use spies.
If you can't see the small subtleties, you won't get the truth
from spies.

⁸Pay attention to small, trifling details!
Spies are helpful in every area.

¹⁰Spies are the first to hear information, so they must not
spread information.
Spies who give your location or talk to others must be killed
along with those to whom they have talked.

Double agents come from converting opponents' information sources, a key source of information about methods.

Unlike the others, doomed spies send information rather than receive it. We use them to communicate a desired impression to others. The general philosophy of doomed spies is to use illusion to control people's perceptions and therefore shape their plans.

Surviving spies are those who return from situations carrying the latest information, telling us the trends.

3 A complete organization is one that is thoroughly informed. In Sun Tzu's view, gathering complete information is a leader's most critical role. It is also one of the best uses for our monetary resources. It must be done quietly so no one knows what we know.

Two characteristics—intelligence and fairness—out of the five qualities of a leader defined in chapter 1 are important in managing information. Intelligence means knowing the ground. Fairness is one of the two organizational "method" qualities.

We must pay attention to the details and gather small bits of information about every area to put together a complete picture.

We must have information sources that we can trust to keep our confidence. While we can't literally kill them if they disappoint us, we must have the courage to stop dealing with those who cannot treat the relationship as confidential.

You may want to attack an army's position. 4
You may want to attack a certain fortification.
You may want to kill people in a certain place.
You must first know the guarding general.
You must know his left and right flanks.
You must know his hierarchy.
You must know the way in.
You must know where different people are stationed.
You must demand this information from your spies.

10You want to know the enemy spies in order to convert
them into your men.
You must find sources of information and bribe them.
You must bring them in with you.
You must obtain them as double agents and use them as
your emissaries.

14Do this correctly and carefully.
You can contact both local and inside spies and obtain their
support.
Do this correctly and carefully.
You create doomed spies by deceiving professionals.
You can use them to give false information.
Do this correctly and carefully.
You must have surviving spies capable of bringing you infor-
mation at the right time.

4 Specific actions or movements, such as attacking a specific person or place, require specific knowledge. We can know generally the methods that we want to employ, but that general knowledge is no substitute for specific information. The specifics that we need to know again follow the five key elements. We need to know the general, his organization, his philosophy, any openings, and his people's positions. To develop this comprehensive picture of a given situation, we must develop conduits of information about that situation.

An "enemy spy," or a reversed conduit, can be anyone that our opponents use as a source of information. The best way to learn about an opponent's best practices is to develop such sources of information. We can simply pay for this information by hiring people away from our competitors. These people connect us to other valuable types of information sources.

Sun Tzu teaches us that building an information network must be done with extreme care. Each step in the process must be accomplished without it becoming general knowledge. The more secretive we can be about our sources of information, the less likely it is that our opponents will be able to tap into them. Even our doomed messengers work more effectively if their connections to us are hidden. If we are quiet and methodical in building up and maintaining our information network, we can have contacts in the key areas of activity that can report the timeliest developments.

²¹These are the five different types of intelligence work.
You must be certain to master them all.
You must be certain to create double agents.
You cannot afford to be too cost conscious in creating these
double agents.

This technique created the success of ancient Shang. 5
This is how the Shang held their dynasty.

³You must always be careful of your success.
Learn from Lu Ya of Shang.

⁵Be a smart commander and a good general.
You do this by using your best and brightest people for spying.
This is how you achieve the greatest success.
This is how you meet the necessities of war.
The whole army's position and ability to move depends on
these spies.

◆ ◆ ◆

◆ ◆ ◆

In modern competition, our most valuable tool is this complete information network. In Sun Tzu's view, it is worth any price because good information can eliminate many of the other costs and much of the waste of competition. The foundation of this network is information sources that we win from the competition.

5 The Shang ruled China from 1600-1050 **B.C.**, just prior to the Zhou dynasty (1050-221 **B.C.**) of Sun Tzu's period.

Whenever Sun Tzu takes lessons from history, he is emphasizing the point that these methods are proven to work over time.

In Sun Tzu's strategy information management is not an ancillary task; it is the core responsibility of any decision-maker. Our best people must be made responsible for it. Information is our source of success. Information gathering can eliminate many of the riskiest and costliest activities of competition. All of our other skills in competition depend upon developing a solid foundation of knowledge.

Related Articles from *Sun Tzu's Playbook*

2.3.5 Infinite Loops: predicting reactions on the basis of the "you-know-that-I-know-that-you-know" problem.

2.3.6 Promises and Threats: the use of promises and threats as strategic moves.

2.4 Contact Networks: the range of contacts needed to create perspective.

2.4.1 Ground Perspective: getting information on a new competitive arena.

2.4.2 Climate Perspective: getting perspective on temporary external conditions.

2.4.3 Command Perspective: developing sources for understanding decision-makers.

2.4.4 Methods Perspective: developing contacts who understand best practices.

2.4.5 Mission Perspective: how we develop and use a perspective on motivation.

2.5 The Big Picture: building big-picture strategic awareness.

2.6 Knowledge Leverage: getting competitive value out of knowledge.

2.7 Information Secrecy: defining the role of secrecy in relationships.

Glossary of Key Strategic Concepts

This glossary is keyed to the most common English words used in the translation of *The Art of War*. Those terms only capture the strategic concepts generally. Though translated as English nouns, verbs, adverbs, or adjectives, the Chinese characters on which they are based are totally conceptual, not parts of speech. For example, the character for CONFLICT is translated as the noun "conflict," as the verb "fight," and as the adjective "disputed." Ancient written Chinese was a conceptual language, not a spoken one. More like mathematical terms, these concepts are primarily defined by the strict structure of their relationships with other concepts. The Chinese names shown in parentheses with the characters are primarily based on Pinyin, but we occasionally use Cantonese terms to make each term unique.

ADVANCE (JEUN 進): to move into new GROUND; to expand your POSITION; to move forward in a campaign; the opposite of FLEE.

ADVANTAGE, *benefit* (LI 利): an opportunity arising from having a better POSITION relative to an ENEMY; an opening left by an ENEMY; a STRENGTH that matches against an ENEMY'S WEAKNESS; where fullness meets emptiness; a desirable characteristic of a strategic POSITION.

AIM, *vision, foresee* (JIAN 見): FOCUS on a specific ADVANTAGE, opening, or opportunity; predicting movements of an ENEMY; a skill of a LEADER in observing CLIMATE.

ANALYSIS, *plan* (GAI 計): a comparison of relative POSITION; the examination of the five factors that define a strategic POSITION; a combination of KNOWLEDGE and VISION; the ability to see through DECEPTION.

ARMY: see WAR.

ATTACK, *invade* (GONG 攻): a movement to new GROUND; advancing a strategic POSITION; action against an ENEMY in the sense of moving into his GROUND; opposite of DEFEND; does not necessarily mean CONFLICT.

BAD, *ruined* (PI 圯): a condition of the GROUND that makes ADVANCE difficult; destroyed; terrain that is broken and difficult to traverse; one of the nine situations or types of terrain.

BARRICADED: see OBSTACLES.

BATTLE (ZHAN 戰): to challenge; to engage an ENEMY; generically, to meet a challenge; to choose a confrontation with an ENEMY at a specific time and place; to focus all your resources on a task; to establish superiority in a POSITION; to challenge an ENEMY to increase CHAOS; that which is CONTROLLED by SURPRISE; one of the

four forms of ATTACK; the response to a DESPERATE SITUATION; character meaning was originally "big meeting," though later took on the meaning "big weapon"; not necessarily CONFLICT.

BRAVERY, *courage* (YONG 勇): the ability to face difficult choices; the character quality that deals with the changes of CLIMATE; courage of conviction; willingness to act on vision; one of the six characteristics of a leader.

BREAK, *broken, divided* (PO 破): to DIVIDE what is COMPLETE; the absence of a UNITING PHILOSOPHY; the opposite of UNITY.

CALCULATE, *count* (SHU 數): mathematical comparison of quantities and qualities; a measurement of DISTANCE or troop size.

CHANGE, *transform* (BIAN 變): transition from one CONDITION to another; the ability to adapt to different situations; a natural characteristic of CLIMATE.

CHAOS, *disorder* (JUAN 亂): CONDITIONS that cannot be FORESEEN; the natural state of confusion arising from BATTLE; one of six weaknesses of an organization; the opposite of CONTROL.

CLAIM, *position, form* (XING 形): to use the GROUND; a shape or specific condition of GROUND; the GROUND that you CONTROL; to use the benefits of the GROUND; the formations of troops; one of the four key skills in making progress.

CLIMATE, *heaven* (TIAN 天): the passage of time; the realm of uncontrollable CHANGE; divine providence; the weather; trends that CHANGE over time; generally, the future; what one must AIM at in the future; one of five key factors in ANALYSIS; the opposite of GROUND.

COMMAND (LING 令): to order or the act of ordering subordinates; the decisions of a LEADER; the creation of METHODS.

COMPETITION: see WAR.

COMPLETE: see UNITY.

CONDITION: see GROUND.

CONFINED, *surround* (WEI 圍): to encircle; a SITUATION or STAGE in which your options are limited; the proper tactic for dealing with an ENEMY that is ten times smaller; to seal off a smaller ENEMY; the characteristic of a STAGE in which a larger FORCE can be attacked by a smaller one; one of nine SITUATIONS or STAGES.

CONFLICT, *fight* (ZHENG 争): to contend; to dispute; direct confrontation of arms with an ENEMY; highly desirable GROUND that creates disputes; one of nine types of GROUND, terrain, or stages.

CONSTRICTED, *narrow* (AI 狹): a confined space or niche; one of six field positions; the limited extreme of the dimension distance; the opposite of SPREAD-OUT.

CONTROL, *govern* (CHI 治): to manage situations; to overcome disorder; the opposite of CHAOS.

DANGEROUS: see SERIOUS.

DANGERS, *adverse* (AK 阨): a condition that makes it difficult to ADVANCE; one of three dimensions used to evaluate advantages; the dimension with the extreme field POSITIONS of ENTANGLING and SUPPORTING.

DEATH, *desperate* (SI 死): to end or the end of life or efforts; an extreme situation in which the only option is BATTLE; one of nine STAGES or types of TERRAIN; one of five types of SPIES; opposite of SURVIVE.

DECEPTION, *bluffing, illusion* (GUI 詭): to control perceptions; to control information; to mislead an ENEMY; an attack on an opponent's AIM; the characteristic of war that confuses perceptions.

DEFEND (SHOU 守): to guard or to hold a GROUND; to remain in a POSITION; the opposite of ATTACK.

DETOUR (YU 迂): the indirect or unsuspected path to a POSITION; the more difficult path to ADVANTAGE; the route that is not DIRECT.

DIRECT, *straight* (JIK 直): a straight or obvious path to a goal; opposite of DETOUR.

DISTANCE, *distant* (YUAN 遠): the space separating GROUND; to be remote from the current location; to occupy POSITIONS that are not close to one another; one of six field positions; one of the three dimensions for evaluating opportunities; the emptiness of space.

DIVIDE, *separate* (FEN 分): to break apart a larger force; to separate from a larger group; the opposite of JOIN and FOCUS.

DOUBLE AGENT, *reverse* (FAN 反): to turn around in direction; to change a situation; to switch a person's allegiance; one of five types of spies.

EASY, *light* (QING 輕): to require little effort; a SITUATION that requires little effort; one of nine STAGES or types of terrain; opposite of SERIOUS.

EMOTION, *feeling* (XIN 心): an unthinking reaction to AIM, a necessary element to inspire MOVES; a component of esprit de corps; never a sufficient cause for ATTACK.

ENEMY, *competitor* (DIK 敵): one who makes the same CLAIM; one with a similar GOAL; one with whom comparisons of capabilities are made.

ENTANGLING, *hanging* (GUA 懸): a POSITION that cannot be returned to; any CONDITION that leaves no easy place to go; one of six field positions.

EVADE, *avoid* (BI 避): the tactic used by small competitors when facing large opponents.

FALL APART, *collapse* (BENG 崩): to fail to execute good decisions; to fail to use a CONSTRICTED POSITION; one of six weaknesses of an organization.

FALL DOWN, *sink* (HAAM 陷): to fail to make good decisions; to MOVE from a SUPPORTING POSITION; one of six weaknesses of organizations.

FEELINGS, *affection, love* (CHING 情): the bonds of relationship; the result of a shared PHILOSOPHY; requires management.

FIGHT, *struggle* (DOU 鬥): to engage in CONFLICT; to face difficulties.

FIRE (HUO 火): an environmental weapon; a universal analogy for all weapons.

FLEE, *retreat, northward* (BEI 北): to abandon a POSITION; to surrender GROUND; one of six weaknesses of an ARMY; opposite of ADVANCE.

FOCUS, *concentrate* (ZHUAN 專): to bring resources together at a given time; to UNITE forces for a purpose; an attribute of having a shared PHILOSOPHY; the opposite of *divide*.

FORCE (LEI 力): power in the simplest sense; a GROUP of people bound by UNITY and FOCUS; the relative balance of STRENGTH in opposition to WEAKNESS.

FORESEE: see AIM.

FULLNESS: see STRENGTH.

GENERAL: see LEADER.

GOAL: see PHILOSOPHY.

GROUND, *situation, stage* (DI 地): the earth; a specific place; a specific condition; the place one competes; the prize of competition; one of five key factors in competitive analysis; the opposite of CLIMATE.

GROUPS, *troops* (DUI 隊): a number of people united under a shared PHILOSOPHY; human resources of an organization; one of the five targets of fire attacks.

INSIDE, *internal* (NEI 內): within a TERRITORY or organization; an insider; one of five types of spies; opposite of OUTSIDE.

INTERSECTING, *highway* (QU 衢): a SITUATION or GROUND that allows you to JOIN; one of nine types of terrain.

JOIN (HAP 合): to unite; to make allies; to create a larger FORCE; opposite of DIVIDE.

KNOWLEDGE, *listening* (ZHI 知): to have information; the result of listening; the first step in advancing a POSITION; the basis of strategy.

LAX, *loosen* (SHII 弛): too easygoing; lacking discipline; one of six weaknesses of an army.

LEADER, *general, commander* (JIANG 將): the decision-maker in a competitive unit; one who LISTENS and AIMS; one who manages TROOPS; superior of officers and men; one of the five key factors in analysis; the conceptual opposite of SYSTEM, the established methods, which do not require decisions.

LEARN, *compare* (XIAO 效): to evaluate the relative qualities of ENEMIES.

LISTEN, *obey* (TING 聽): to gather KNOWLEDGE; part of ANALYSIS.

LISTENING: see KNOWLEDGE.

LOCAL, *countryside* (XIANG 鄉): the nearby GROUND; to have KNOWLEDGE of a specific GROUND; one of five types of SPIES.

MARSH (ZE 澤): GROUND where footing is unstable; one of the four types of GROUND; analogy for uncertain situations.

METHOD: see SYSTEM.

MISSION: see PHILOSOPHY.

MOMENTUM, *influence* (SHI 勢): the FORCE created by SURPRISE set up by STANDARDS; used with TIMING.

MOUNTAINS, *hill, peak* (SHAN 山): uneven GROUND; one of four types of GROUND; an analogy for all unequal SITUATIONS.

MOVE, *march, act* (HANG 行): action toward a position or goal.

NATION (GUO 國): the state; the productive part of an organization; the seat of political power; the entity that controls an ARMY or competitive part of the organization.

OBSTACLES, *barricaded* (XIAN 險): to have barriers; one of the three characteristics of the GROUND; one of six field positions; as a field position, opposite of UNOBSTRUCTED.

OPEN, *meeting, crossing* (JIAO 來): to share the same GROUND without conflict; to come together; a SITUATION that encourages a race; one of nine TERRAINS or STAGES.

OPPORTUNITY: see ADVANTAGE.

OUTMANEUVER (SOU 走): to go astray; to be FORCED into a WEAK POSITION; one of six weaknesses of an army.

OUTSIDE, *external* (WAI 外): not within a TERRITORY or ARMY; one who has a different perspective; one who offers an objective view; opposite of INTERNAL.

PHILOSOPHY, *mission, goals* (TAO 道): the shared GOALS that UNITE an ARMY; a system of thought; a shared viewpoint; literally "the way"; a way to work together; one of the five key factors in ANALYSIS.

PLATEAU (LIU 陸): a type of GROUND without defects; an analogy for any equal, solid, and certain SITUATION; the best place for competition; one of the four types of GROUND.

RESOURCES, *provisions* (LIANG 糧): necessary supplies, most commonly food; one of the five targets of fire attacks.

RESTRAINT: see TIMING.

REWARD, *treasure, money* (BAO 賞): profit; wealth; the necessary compensation for competition; a necessary ingredient for

VICTORY; VICTORY must pay.

SCATTER, *dissipating* (SAN 散): to disperse; to lose UNITY; the pursuit of separate GOALS as opposed to a central MISSION; a situation that causes a FORCE to scatter; one of nine conditions or types of terrain.

SERIOUS, *heavy* (CHONG 重): any task requiring effort and skill; a SITUATION where resources are running low when you are deeply committed to a campaign or heavily invested in a project; a situation where opposition within an organization mounts; one of nine STAGES or types of TERRAIN.

SIEGE (GONG CHENG 攻城): to move against entrenched positions; any movement against an ENEMY'S STRENGTH; literally "strike city"; one of the four forms of attack; the least desirable form of attack.

SITUATION: see GROUND.

SPEED, *hurry* (SAI 馳): to MOVE over GROUND quickly; the ability to ADVANCE POSITIONS in a minimum of time; needed to take advantage of a window of opportunity.

SPREAD-OUT, *wide* (GUANG 廣): a surplus of DISTANCE; one of the six GROUND POSITIONS; opposite of CONSTRICTED.

SPY, *conduit, go-between* (GAAN 間): a source of information; a channel of communication; literally, an "opening between."

STAGE: see GROUND.

STANDARD, *proper, correct* (JANG 正): the expected behavior; the standard approach; proven methods; the opposite of SURPRISE; together with SURPRISE creates MOMENTUM.

STOREHOUSE, *house* (KU 庫): a place where resources are stockpiled; one of the five targets for fire attacks.

STORES, *accumulate, savings* (JI 糧): resources that have been stored; any type of inventory; one of the five targets of fire attacks.

STRENGTH, *fullness, satisfaction* (SAT 壹): wealth or abundance or resources; the state of being crowded; the opposite of XU, empty.

SUPPLY WAGONS, *transport* (ZI 輜): the movement of RESOURCES through DISTANCE; one of the five targets of fire attacks.

SUPPORT, *supporting* (ZHII 支): to prop up; to enhance; a GROUND POSITION that you cannot leave without losing STRENGTH; one of six field positions; the opposite extreme of ENTANGLING.

SURPRISE, *unusual, strange* (QI 奇): the unexpected; the innovative; the opposite of STANDARD; together with STANDARDS creates MOMENTUM.

SURROUND: see CONFINED.

SURVIVE, *live, birth* (SHAANG 生): the state of being created, started, or beginning; the state of living or surviving; a temporary condition of fullness; one of five types of spies; the opposite of DEATH.

SYSTEM, *method* (FA 法): a set of procedures; a group of techniques; steps to accomplish a GOAL; one of the five key factors in analysis; the realm of groups who must follow procedures; the opposite of the LEADER.

TERRITORY, *terrain*: see GROUND.

TIMING, *restraint* (JIE 節): to withhold action until the proper time; to release tension; a companion concept to MOMENTUM.

TROOPS: see GROUPS.

UNITY, *whole, oneness* (YI 一): the characteristic of a GROUP that shares a PHILOSOPHY; the lowest number; a GROUP that acts as a unit; the opposite of DIVIDED.

UNOBSTRUCTED, *expert* (TONG 通): without obstacles or barriers; GROUND that allows easy movement; open to new ideas; one of six field positions; opposite of OBSTRUCTED.

VICTORY, *win, winning* (SING 勝): success in an endeavor; getting a reward; serving your mission; an event that produces more than it consumes; to make a profit.

WAR, *competition, army* (BING 兵): a dynamic situation in which POSITIONS can be won or lost; a contest in which a REWARD can be won; the conditions under which the rules of strategy work.

WATER, *river* (SHUI 水): a fast-changing GROUND; fluid CONDITIONS; one of four types of GROUND; an analogy for change.

WEAKNESS, *emptiness, need* (XU 虛): the absence of people or resources; devoid of FORCE; the point of ATTACK for an ADVANTAGE; a characteristic of GROUND that enables SPEED; poor; the opposite of STRENGTH.

WIN, *winning*: see VICTORY.

WIND, *fashion, custom* (FENG 風): the pressure of environmental forces.

Index of Topics in *The Art of War*

This index identifies significant topics, keyed to the chapters, block numbers (big numbers in text), and line numbers (tiny numbers). The format is chapter:block.lines.

About the Author

Gary Gagliardi

This book's award-winning translator and primary author, Gary Gagliardi, is America's leading authority on Sun Tzu's *The Art of War*. A frequent guest on radio and television talk shows, Gary has written over wenty books on strategy. Ten of his books on Sun Tzu's methods have won award recognition in business, self-help, career, sports, philosophy, multicultural, and youth nonfiction categories.

Gary began studying Sun Tzu's philosophy over thirty years ago. His understanding of strategy was proven in the business world, where his software company became one of the Inc. 500 fastest-growing companies in America and won numerous business awards. After selling his software company, Gary began writing about and teaching Sun Tzu's strategic philosophy full time.

He has spoken all over the world on a variety of topics concerning competition, from modern technology to ancient history. His books have been translated into many languages, including Japanese, Thai, Korean, Russian, Indonesian, and Spanish.

Today he splits his time between Seattle and Las Vegas, living with his wife, Rebecca, and travels extensively for speaking engagements all over the world.

garyg@suntzus.com

@strategygary

Want to learn more about Sun Tzu's Strategy?
There is Much,Much More....

SUNTZUS.COM

‎IENCE OF STRATEGY INSTITUTE

eBooks

Audio books

Audio seminars

Online training

Art of War and Strategy Books By Gary Gagliardi

Sun Tzu's Art of War Rule Book in Nine Volumes

Sun Tzu's The Art of War Plus The Art of Sales: Strategy for the Sales Warrior

9 Formulas for Business Success: the Science of Strategy

The Golden Key to Strategy: Everyday Strategy for Everyone

The Art of War Plus The Chinese Revealed

The Art of War Plus The Art of Management: Straegy for Management Warriors

Art of War for Warrior Marketing: Strategy for Conquering Markets

The Art of War Plus The Art of Politics: Strategy for Campaigns (with Shawn Frost)

Making Money By Speaking: The Spokesperson Strategy

The Warrior Class: 306 Lessons in Strategy

The Art of War for the Business Warrior: Strategy for Entrepreneurs

The Art of War Plus The Warrior's Apprentice: Strategy for Teens

The Art of War Plus Strategy for Sales Managers: Strategy for Sales Groups

The Ancient Bing-fa: Martial Arts Strategy

Strategy Against Terror: Ancient Wisdom for Today's War

The Art of War Plus The Art of Career Building: Strategy for Promotion

Sun Tzu's Art of War Plus Parenting Teens

The Art of War Plus Its Amazing Secrets: The Keys to Ancient Chinese Science

Art of War Plus Art of Love: Strategy for Romance

Made in the USA
San Bernardino, CA
07 November 2017